Excel Basics

In 30 Minutes

The beginner's guide to Excel, Excel Online, and Google Sheets

SECOND EDITION

Ian Lamont

Original interior design by Monica Thomas for TLC Graphics, www.TLCGraphics.com. Interior design assisted and composition by Rick Soldin, book-comp.com.

Contents

Excel:
not just for nerds!

Some years ago, a colleague stopped by my cubicle and asked for help with a project he was working on. John wanted to create a long list of names, categorize them, and assign a score on a scale of one to 10 for each one. He also needed to identify the top scores and create category averages.

John knew I was familiar with all kinds of desktop and online software. He asked, "Which one would you recommend for these types of tasks?"

"That's easy," I answered. "Enter the data into Microsoft Excel or Google Sheets. You can then alphabetize the list, sort by the highest and lowest scores, and draw out category averages. You can even create neat-looking charts based on the results." I used Excel to whip up a basic list, and emailed him the file.

John thanked me profusely, but admitted, "I have only the vaguest idea about Excel and almost no experience with spreadsheets."

John's situation is not unusual. Millions of people know that Excel can be used for financial tracking and number crunching. They may have even opened Excel and entered some numbers into a corporate expense worksheet.

Nevertheless, Excel suffers from an *image problem.* Most people assume that spreadsheet programs such as Excel are intended for accountants, analysts, financiers, scientists, mathematicians, and other geeky types. Creating a spreadsheet, sorting data, using functions, and making charts seems daunting. Many think that these are tasks best left to the nerds.

I'm here to tell you that spreadsheets are not just for nerds. Almost anyone can use Excel for work, school, personal projects and other uses. I've written this guide to help you quickly get up to speed on basic concepts, using plain English, step-by-step instructions, and lots of screenshots. Thirty minutes from now, you'll know how to:

➤ Create a spreadsheet and enter numbers and text into cells.

➤ Perform addition, multiplication, and other simple mathematical functions.

➤ Derive values based on percentages.

➤ Perform timesaving tasks, such as sorting large lists and automatically applying the same formula across a range of values.

➤ Make great-looking charts.

You can imagine how these techniques can help in real-world situations, from tracking household expenses to making sales projections. You can even use them to organize events, and track the office football pool.

We only have 30 minutes, so let's get started!

CHAPTER 1

The basics: cells, functions, and formulas

Like John, I never touched a spreadsheet until well into adulthood. Even though I had Excel and other spreadsheet programs on my work and personal computers, I didn't attempt to learn how they worked. Spreadsheets seemed alien and hard to use.

Consider Microsoft Excel. This popular spreadsheet program is nothing like word processors or email, which start with open writing areas to enter text. A spreadsheet presents a giant grid of unmarked rectangles called cells, which are identified by a combination of letters and numbers (for instance, "B3" or "AA34"). You have to type functions that use some sort of secret code instead of plain English. For example, "=SUM(A3:A5)" is used for addition, instead of numbers and a plus symbol. There are many other bizarre aspects of Excel. It even uses Greek for some commands!

A project at work was the catalyst to learn how to use Excel. I was employed by a local university, and one day I was given a long list of names and the fees each person had paid for class reunions and other activities. I knew it would take hours to add everything up with a calculator. I also had to sort the lists to show who had paid the most in each class. My supervisor, seeing how anxious I was, suggested using Excel. Standing over my shoulder, she demystified spreadsheets for me, and showed me how a spreadsheet could be a huge timesaver.

Over the next half-hour, I want to demystify spreadsheets for you. Instead of using a boring old alumni list, we'll turn to a training exercise: You'll be responsible for tracking the monthly earnings of Jennifer, Curtis, and Kara, who all work in the sales department. It's January, and you're going to calculate their projected earnings through June. You will even create a nifty chart to show your boss. And, after discovering that two people on the sales team have some quirky personal issues, you'll work out some alternative earnings scenarios.

The different flavors of Excel (and Google Sheets)

The second edition of *Excel Basics In 30 Minutes* has been updated to cover the most recent versions of Excel. While the book is intended for people who want to learn how to use Microsoft Excel, I am also including instructions for Google Sheets, an online spreadsheets program that is part of the Google Drive Web-based office suite. The reason: Not all readers of this guide want to invest more than $100 to buy a copy of Microsoft Office or start a paid subscription to Office 365. Google Sheets is free, and if you decide to purchase Excel or Microsoft Office later, the core techniques you've learned with Sheets will carry over to Excel.

If you are using Excel, there are many different current and legacy versions of the software. Here are the versions you are most likely to encounter:

Excel 2003 (and earlier), Excel for Mac (2008 or earlier)

Older PCs or Macs may have an outdated version of Excel. This is not a huge drawback, as older versions of Excel are very powerful tools that are perfectly capable of crunching data and generating simple charts. However, there are some issues to be aware of:

1. Important features and toggles tend to be deeply buried in menus, which may slow you down.

2. When saving a spreadsheet file, older versions may use the .xls file extension, as opposed to the newer .xlsx format. While newer, paid

versions of Excel can still open .xls files, a free online version of Excel called Excel Online may have trouble opening certain .xls files.

3. Chart options are usually quite basic.

4. Saving spreadsheets to OneDrive, Microsoft's online storage service, may not work for older versions of Excel.

Note that interfaces for older versions of Excel may not match up with the instructions given later in this guide.

Recent versions of Excel (up to Excel 2016)

Starting with Office 2007 for PCs, and Office for Mac 2011, Microsoft introduced a new *ribbon* interface in Excel. It provides a much more visual way of navigating spreadsheets and spreadsheet tools—for instance, to change the number format from dollars to percent, all you need to do is press the % button on the Home ribbon, instead of hunting through menus for the right setting. In addition, Mac users will find Excel 2016 now looks and behaves like its Windows counterpart, down to many keyboard shortcuts which now work on both operating systems.

While there are slight variations between the ribbon interfaces on newer versions of Excel, most of the instructions in *Excel Basics In 30 Minutes* apply to Excel 2010, Excel 2013, and Excel 2016. In addition, Users of Excel 2016 now have new options to save and share workbooks using OneDrive and other online storage services, which allow for easier collaboration.

Office 2016 vs. Office 365

Customers can purchase Office 2016, which contains Excel 2016, Word 2016, and PowerPoint 2016. However, it is also possible to use the subscription-based Office 365, which lets users pay a monthly fee for access to the latest versions of Excel, Word, and other programs in the Microsoft Office suite.

There are different versions of Office 365 for home and business users with various cost and licensing structures. I use the least expensive subscription tier which allows installation on one desktop computer and one mobile device and a limited amount of free storage space on OneDrive. However, it is possible to purchase family or business subscriptions which permit more installations and users to access Office.

Besides the subscription requirement, there are other important differences between Office 365 and earlier versions of Microsoft Office:

➤ Office 365 is tightly integrated with Microsoft's online file storage service, OneDrive, but users also have the option of storing documents on another online service, Dropbox.

➤ Office 365 is automatically upgraded with new features and new versions of the software over time, whereas desktop versions of Office will only receive normal product updates and bug fixes for that version.

➤ I have noticed registration errors when my computer or device is not connected to the Internet. This can reduce the functionality of Excel, and limit the ability to save to OneDrive and other online services.

To start a subscription, visit *office.microsoft.com* and select Office 365. You will need to register for the service, activate the subscription, and download and install the entire office suite, which includes the most recent version of Excel. It is possible to turn off the subscription if you do not anticipate using it for a few months, and then reactivate it later.

Excel Online

Microsoft has copied Google's approach to online office suites, and now offers a free version of Excel that can be accessed via Internet Explorer, Firefox, and other Web browsers.

As a free tool, Excel Online includes basic spreadsheet tools and functionality. Excel Online uses a stripped-down ribbon interface. Like Google Sheets, Excel Online makes it possible to share spreadsheets with other users, or embed a spreadsheet on a Web page.

Registration is easy. All you need to do is go to *office.com* and follow the instructions to start using Office Online. You'll need a Microsoft Account, which you may already have if you use other Microsoft products (I was able to log in using my Xbox Live credentials). Files created in Excel Online will be saved to OneDrive, an online storage service that is similar to Dropbox or Google Drive.

While Excel Online is free, it comes up short in a few important areas:

➤ Excel Online requires a live Internet connection, while Google Sheets allows users to work offline under certain circumstances (see Google Sheets' help resources or Chapter 7 of *Google Drive & Docs In 30 Minutes* for more information).

➤ Sophisticated formatting of spreadsheet data is not possible with Excel Online.

➤ Users can create charts in Excel Online, but the appearance is very basic, and there aren't many customization options.

➤ Excel Online cannot filter data, track changes, insert pictures, or handle other advanced features.

➤ Older .xls files may not open in Excel Online, and it's not possible to import common data formats such as text files containing comma-separated values.

For these reasons, I recommend sticking with Google Sheets, which is free and has a much more complete feature set. If you want to try Excel Online, go to office.com, select *Excel Online*, and log in or register using a Microsoft Account.

Excel for mobile devices

It's possible to download Excel to run on phones and tablets that use iOS, Android, or Windows, via the mobile Office apps. Mobile Office apps are free for personal use. However, the functionality of Excel on mobile devices is limited. Many of the exercises in this guide cannot be performed on a phone or tablet version of Excel, so it's best to use a desktop version of Excel or Google Sheets when following along.

Google Sheets

Google Sheets is part of Google Drive, the free online storage and office suite available at *drive.google.com*. For basic spreadsheet needs, Sheets is a fine alternative to Excel and offers more functionality than Excel Online, the competing free product offered by Microsoft. Appendix I explains how to register for a Google Account to use Google Sheets.

Using this guide with Excel and Google Sheets

When it comes to spreadsheet basics, the various flavors of Excel and Google Sheets are quite similar in terms of the appearance of worksheets and how common tasks are carried out. Assume instructions are applicable to recent versions of Excel and Google Sheets unless stated otherwise. Note that the instructions in this book may not always match up with what you see on the screen, owing to regular software updates and interface upgrades. On the official website for this book (*excel.in30minutes.com*), you'll find sample spreadsheets and video tutorials to reinforce the lessons in this book.

One last thing before we dive into spreadsheets: The purpose of this guide is to explain the basics, covering those skills that I believe will benefit you most as a learner and user. It is not intended to be a comprehensive guide. Further, I am not making any guarantees that you will be able to take over your company's accounting department, much less make error-free work-sheets. Nevertheless, 30 minutes from now, you will hopefully have learned some core spreadsheet skills... and even a trick or two!

Firing up Excel and creating a new file

If you have Excel installed on your PC or Mac, open it now:

Windows: *Start > Excel*

Mac/OS X: *Finder > Applications > Microsoft Excel*

Office Online: *Go to office.com*, log on with your Microsoft credentials, and select *Excel Online*

If you don't have Microsoft Excel, use the free online spreadsheet program offered by Google, known as Google Sheets. You will need to register a Google Account by visiting *drive.google.com* (see Appendix I for instructions on how to register).

Once you've opened Excel or Sheets, create a new spreadsheet file and name it *Monthly Earnings:*

➤ **Excel:** *File > New* to open Excel's *Backstage View* screen (see screenshot, below). Select *Blank Workbook* from the available templates and press *Create.*

➤ **Google Sheets:** Go to *drive.google.com* and then select *New > Google Sheets.* Select the default name at the top of the browser window to rename it.

Creating a new spreadsheet file in Excel:

If you are away from your PC or laptop, read through this section and refer to the included screenshots.

Spreadsheet terminology

Microsoft uses the term *workbooks* to describe spreadsheet files in Excel. Google Sheets does not use this term. Throughout this book, I will use "spreadsheet file" to refer to files.

The grid that you see in front of you is called a *worksheet.* A spreadsheet file can have more than one worksheet, and they will be layered on top of each other and accessed via tabs at the bottom of the grid (we'll explore how to create new worksheets later). Here's what a worksheet looks like in Excel:

Google Sheets:

If you're using Microsoft Excel, you may see a split screen, which is the Page Layout view. To see everything on one sheet, go to the View ribbon and select *Normal.*

What the different ribbons do

The Excel interface includes numerous top-level ribbons. Access the following features by switching ribbons:

➤ **Home**. Text/cell formatting, number formats, text wrapping, insert or delete cells/rows/columns, AutoSum and other basic functions, basic sorting and filtering (see screenshot, below).

➤ **Insert**. Pivot tables, images, shapes, charts, links, comments, headers and footers, mathematical equations, symbols and emojis.

➤ **Page Layout**. Themes, margins, portrait or landscape, size, print area, gridlines, headings.

➤ **Formulas**. Insert, AutoSum, financial, logical, text, date & time, lookup & reference, math, trace precedents, trace dependents, error checking, calculation options.

➤ **Data**. Import and database options, sort, filter, validation, group/ungroup, subtotal.

➤ **Review**. Spelling, thesaurus, comments, track changes, security options.

➤ **View**. On-screen layout, zoom, gridlines, Formula Bar, freeze panes, split view, macros.

➤ **Contextual**. Additional ribbons may appear depending on the context, such as the Chart Design ribbon which appears when working with charts.

Excel Online uses a smaller number of ribbons with a greatly reduced feature set. Google Sheets uses a single formatting toolbar, with additional features accessed via menus.

Working with cells

The small rectangles that fill a worksheet are called cells. They are designed to hold numbers (for instance, 5, 26.2, $500 or 98%) as well as text ("Sarah", "Account past due", "245-BNX", column headers, etc.). Sometimes, people will use a cell to refer to other cells that are part of a formula (more on that in a few minutes).

Because there are so many cells, worksheets use a simple system to identify each one. The top of each column is labeled with letters, while the rows running down the left side of the window are labeled with numbers. It's just like the game Battleship, in which you identify a specific location on the grid by calling out "A7" or "J3". If the worksheet has more than 26 columns, the 27th column is labeled AA, the 28th column is labeled AB, etc.

You can use arrow keys or sliders to move quickly around the worksheet.

Your first spreadsheet formula

Let's do a quick exercise. On the new spreadsheet you've just created, find cell A2. It should be the second cell from the top of column A. In it, type the name "Jennifer", and press *Return/Enter*. You should see this:

If a few of the letters are cut off, don't worry—the cell still contains the entire name. It's easy to make the cell larger. A cell's width (and the width of all of the other cells in the same column) can be adjusted by hovering the mouse over the dividing line between two cells until a cursor with two tiny left-right arrows appears (see screenshot, below). The dividing line between the cells can then be grabbed and dragged to the right until the entire word appears.

	A		B	C	D	E	
		Width: 11.27 (131 pixels)					
1							
2	Jennifer						
3							
4							
5							
6							
7							

In cell B1, type "January". This is the header for column B, which will display the monthly earnings for each person on the team.

Select cell B2. Type "$5000" and hit *Return/Enter.* The cells should like this:

	A	B	C	D	E
1		January			
2	Jennifer	$5,000			
3					
4					
5					
6					
7					
8					
9					

In cell A3 (below "Jennifer") type a new name: Curtis. In cell B3, type "$5500". In cell A4 and B4, add "Kara" and "$5425". Your worksheet should now look like this:

	A	B	C	D	E	F
1		January				
2	Jennifer	$5,000				
3	Curtis	$5,500				
4	Kara	$5,425				
5						
6						

Let's say we wanted to add up these amounts to determine how much money the group collectively earns. Doing the addition in our heads would be slow, and we might make mistakes. Doing it with a pen and paper would be time-consuming. But spreadsheets make it easy, using three different methods:

➤ A formula featuring the addition symbol.

➤ The SUM function.

➤ The *AutoSum* button.

Let's first use the addition symbol in a worksheet formula to calculate the collective earnings of the three colleagues. This requires selecting an empty cell that will calculate the total of the three cells. It can be the cell immediately below the numbers, or it can be a cell that's located several columns away. The calculation can be completed anywhere on the worksheet, and will refer back to the cells that contain the values to be added together.

Let's select a cell two columns over—cell D6. In it, type the following text. But don't press *Return/Enter* yet:

$$=B2+B3+B4$$

This is a *formula*. All formulas and functions entered into a spreadsheet have to start with an equal sign ("="). It looks backwards, but starting with an equal sign tells Excel or Sheets that you are entering a formula or function, as opposed to typing text or numbers.

B2, B3, and B4 are references to the cells that contain the dollar amounts associated with Jennifer, Curtis, and Kara. References can be typed as lowercase ("b3") but spreadsheet programs will convert them to uppercase.

As you type each reference into your formula, the cell in question will have a colored rectangle drawn around it. The color of the text being typed changes color to match it:

The colored outlines verify that you are typing the correct cell references. For instance, if you mistakenly typed C3 instead of B3, an empty cell would be highlighted, instantly letting you know that you had entered the wrong cell reference.

As you type, you may also notice that the *Formula Bar* at the top of the screen shows exactly what you are typing:

SUM	▾ ⋮ ✕ ✓ *fx*	=B2+B3+B4		
◢	A	B	C	D
1		January		
2	Jennifer	$5,000		
3	Curtis	$5,500		
4	Kara	$5,425		
5				
6				=B2+B3+B4
7				

Press the *Return/Enter* key. The result of adding the three cells is shown in cell D6. Move the mouse to cell D6 and select it again. The number in the cell stays the same, but the Formula Bar still displays the formula you entered. This is a handy way of determining how a cell's value was calculated.

Introducing functions with SUM

Let's say you want to perform addition on 10 cells. Would you want to type something like this?

=B2+B3+B4+B5+B6+B7+B8+B9+B10+B11

Probably not. It not only takes a long time to type, it's also easy to make a mistake.

There's another way to perform addition, using the SUM function and a range of cells.

Let's demonstrate on the same set of data. This time, we'll place the answer in a different cell, so we can see the results side by side. Select cell C6. In it, type the following text (but don't press *Return/Enter* yet):

$$=SUM(B2:B4)$$

This is what you should see:

SUM	▾	× ✓ *fx*	=SUM(B2:B4)			
	A	**B**	**C**	**D**	**E**	
1		January				
2	Jennifer	$5,000				
3	Curtis	$5,500				
4	Kara	$5,425				
5						
6			=SUM(B2:B4)	$15,925		

SUM() is a *function*. In spreadsheet programs, functions perform specific tasks. It could be a mathematical operation such as subtraction or division, a data transformation, or some other specialized process.

As with the formula we performed earlier, functions always start with an equal sign. "SUM" is the name of the function. Think of SUM as an addition robot that adds together whatever is inside the parentheses that follow. The text inside the parentheses—"B2:B4"—tells Excel to include the entire range of values that start with cell B2 and end with cell B4. In other words, it is the sum of the values in cells B2, B3, and B4.

Press *Return*. The sum of the three cells is shown in cell C6, next to the same value shown in cell D6. The methods are different, but the result is the same:

C7	▾	× ✓ *fx*				
	A	**B**	**C**	**D**	**E**	
1		January				
2	Jennifer	$5,000				
3	Curtis	$5,500				
4	Kara	$5,425				
5						
6			$15,925	$15,925		
7						

The SUM function requires numerical values. For instance, typing "=SUM(A2:A4)" in the Monthly Earnings spreadsheet would result in zero, or an error message. Why? Because the contents of cells A2, A3, and A4 are the names of people, and letters cannot be added.

AutoSum and the one Greek letter you need to know

There's one more way to perform addition that is even easier than the two methods just described. Remember the buttons with Greek letters, mentioned at the beginning of this chapter? Greek is used by mathematicians, scientists, economists, and other brainy types to write equations and other mathematical concepts. The Greek letter Sigma, which looks a little like a capital "M" turned on its side, represents the AutoSum function in Excel. Look for this button on the Home or Formulas ribbons:

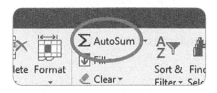

If you select a series of numbers and press the *AutoSum* button on the Home ribbon, the next cell after the series will show the total.

Let's try it on the amounts assigned to our friends Jennifer, Curtis, and Kara. Click down on cell B2, but don't release the mouse button. While holding down the button, move the mouse down until cells B3 and B4 are also selected. Then release the mouse button. It should look like this:

	A	B	C	D	E	F	G
1		January					
2	Jennifer	$5,000					
3	Curtis	$5,500					
4	Kara	$5,425					
5							
6			$15,925	$15,925			
7							

Next, press *AutoSum*. The total is shown in cell B5.

	A	B	C	D	E	F
1		January				
2	Jennifer	$5,000				
3	Curtis	$5,500				
4	Kara	$5,425				
5		$15,925				
6			$15,925	$15,925		
7						
8	Σ AutoSum			=SUM(B2:B4)	=B2+B3+B4	
9						

(Formula bar: B2 ... fx 5000)

Quickly accessing other functions

Look for the small triangle next to the Sigma button and select it. A small menu of options will appear. This is an easy way to select commonly used functions. The next function on the list, *Average*, shows the average of the selected cells. If you select *More Functions*, you'll be able to choose from hundreds of other functions that do everything from displaying today's date to calculating financial results.

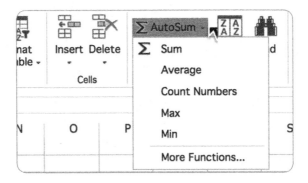

Google Sheets also contains a Sigma button. Pressing it does not perform the AutoSum function—it simply displays the available functions, including SUM:

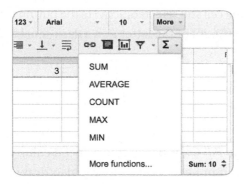

Formatting cells and text

There's one more basic lesson, and then you'll be ready to continue to the next chapter. This lesson explains how to format text and cells, using the formatting options on the Home ribbon in Excel:

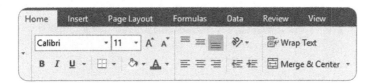

Google Sheets doesn't use ribbons, but rather has a single toolbar that includes formatting options:

The formatting options can be very useful if you want to change the appearance of text or values, organize the contents of a spreadsheet for easier viewing, or highlight an important cell or group of cells.

Using the example, let's make the column and row headers stand out:

1. Start by highlighting cell B1 ("January")
2. Press the button that has the letter "B" on it. This will bold the text.

3. Then, with the cell still selected, activate the button that looks like a tiny paint bucket (Excel) or the letter A in a dark square (Google Sheets):

This determines the *Fill Color* of the cell. Select a color you like. It's useful for highlighting column headers, and it will also draw people's attention when it is printed out (see Chapter 4).

While we're at it, let's change the typeface (also known as the font) for the column header and the size of the letters. The default font style is Arial, but let's pick something else. To change the font, first select cell B1. Then, select the drop-down menu next to the *Font* field and scroll through the list of fonts until something interesting or appropriate turns up. There are many choices:

For this example, let's choose *Times New Roman*. The column headers now look like this:

The header text is too small, so the font size needs to be bumped up. Select the column header (cell B1). The *Font Size* selector displays the number 10, which applies 10-point type to the selected text. That's too small. Select the *Font Size* drop-down menu next to the number 10, and select 12. It makes the column headers stand out much more clearly. It now looks like this:

	A	B	C	D	E	F
1		January				
2	Jennifer	$5,000				
3	Curtis	$5,500				
4	Kara	$5,425				
5		$15,925				
6			$15,925			
7						
8						

Bolding the text helps column headers stand out:

	A	B	C	D	E	F
1		**January**				
2	Jennifer	$5,000				
3	Curtis	$5,500				
4	Kara	$5,425				
5		$15,925				
6			$15,925			
7						

There's one more thing to do: Clean up the bottom cells. Erase the totals in cells C6 and D6 by highlighting them and selecting *Edit > Clear > Contents*, or right-clicking and selecting *Clear Contents*. In Google Sheets, just press the *Delete* button on the keyboard.

Using templates and themes

Templates are premade spreadsheet designs that you can use for new Excel and Google Sheets projects. Examples include to-do lists, budget spreadsheets, and loan calculators. Themes are preset styles and color combinations that you can apply to existing spreadsheets in Excel.

How to create a new spreadsheet file based on a template

Excel:

➤ Select *File > New* or *File > New from Template* and choose from one of the available templates (scroll down to see them all).

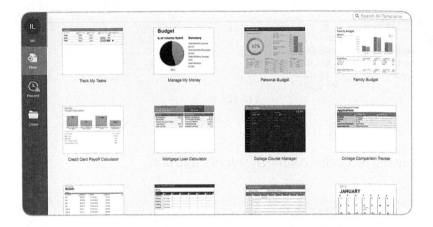

Excel Online:

➤ *File > New* and select one of the available templates.

Google Sheets:

➤ Select a template from the main Google Sheets screen.

➤ Select *File > New > From template.*

How to create a new template in Excel

1. From an open spreadsheet file, select *File > Save as Template*.

2. Give the template a name, and make sure the file format is Excel Template (.xltx).

   Note: This option is not available in Excel Online.

How to apply themes in Excel

Themes are preset font and color combinations that you can apply to existing spreadsheets:

➤ Go to the Page Layout ribbon and press the *Themes* button to see available font and color options. Click to select.

➤ To change the colors but not the fonts, press the *Colors* button on the Page Layout ribbon.

➤ To change the fonts but not the colors, press the *Fonts* button on the Page Layout ribbon.

➤ Themes are not currently available in Excel Online or Google Sheets.

For a new blank spreadsheet file, Excel will apply a default theme (the default theme colors are visible when you apply a background color to selected cells from the Home ribbon).

Chapter quiz

The following questions are based on the material learned in the first chapter, but in a few cases you'll have to deduce how to proceed.

1. Using Microsoft Excel or Google Sheets, demonstrate at least two ways to add the numbers 64, 22.5, 13 and 2.

2. How would you calculate the average earnings of Jennifer, Curtis, and Kara in January?

3. How can the background color of a group of cells be changed?

Answers can be found in Appendix II on page 93.

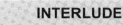

Excel Ninja skill #1: AutoFill

We've covered some important basics. Now it's time to have a little fun. This interlude covers AutoFill, an important spreadsheet feature that can save loads of time and amaze your friends (well, at least some of them).

If you're committed to learning how to use spreadsheets, AutoFill is a very important skill to learn. Think of AutoFill as the *shuriken* (Japanese throwing star) of spreadsheets. This simple act, which entails dragging the pointer horizontally or vertically across cells, has great power in the hands of those who know how to use it. AutoFill works in Excel, Excel Online, and Google Sheets.

AutoFill magic

The best way to illustrate what AutoFill can do is to try it out. Let's return to the Monthly Earnings spreadsheet that we started earlier.

1. Select cell B1. This is the cell that contains "January."

2. Hover the mouse pointer over the lower right corner of the high-lighted cell until you see a small square dot or crosshair. Grab it with your mouse, and drag five cells to the right (see screenshot, below).

3. Release the mouse button.

B1	▾ : × ✓ ƒx	January					
◢	A	**B**	**C**	**D**	**E**	**F**	▴
1		**January**	**February**	**March**	**April**	**May**	
2	Jennifer	$5,000					⊞
3	Curtis	$5,500					
4	Kara	$5,425					
5		$15,925					
6							
7							

The spreadsheet automatically typed the names of the other months, and added the formatting used for January!

Note that some spreadsheet programs, including Google Sheets, require two cells in a series to be highlighted in order for AutoFill to complete the series:

1. B1 contains "January."

2. Type "February" in cell C1.

3. Highlight both cells simultaneously (you can do this by selecting cell B1 but not letting go, and sliding the mouse over to C1 before releasing the button).

4. Hover over the lower right corner of cell C1, until crosshairs or a dot appears.

5. Grab the crosshairs with your mouse and drag right until you get to cell G1. Then let go.

Formulas and AutoFill

AutoFill also works with numbers in a series. It can automatically calculate a trend, based on existing numbers on a worksheet. Two adjacent cells in the same row are all you need.

Let's try it out with the Monthly Earnings spreadsheet file. Jennifer's earnings are predicted to rise $50 per month through June, as she steadily increases her commissions. In January, her earnings were $5,000. Type "$5050" for her February earnings (cell C2). Then, highlight her earnings for January and February:

	A	B	C	D	E	F
1		January	February	March	April	May
2	Jennifer	$5,000	$5,050			
3	Curtis	$5,500				
4	Kara	$5,425				
5		$15,925				
6						
7						

Hover over the lower right corner, and grab the dot/crosshair that appears. Drag it to column G. Releasing it, this is what we see:

	A	B	C	D	E	F
1		January	February	March	April	May
2	Jennifer	$5,000	$5,050	$5,100	$5,150	$5,200
3	Curtis	$5,500				
4	Kara	$5,425				
5		$15,925				
6						
7						

The spreadsheet adds $50 each month to Jennifer's earnings, without having to type any formulas or functions.

It's possible to drag more than one row at a time. Let's say Curtis' earnings are predicted to decline $100 per month. It turns out he cares less and less about this sales job because he's preoccupied with his dreams of becoming a professional chef! Meanwhile, Kara's earnings are rising a mere $7 per month. In cell C3, which represent Curtis' earnings for February, type "$5400". In cell C4, which shows Kara's projected earnings for February, type "$5432". This is what should be on the screen:

	A	B	C	D	E	F
1		January	February	March	April	May
2	Jennifer	$5,000	$5,050	$5,100	$5,150	$5,200
3	Curtis	$5,500	$5,400			
4	Kara	$5,425	$5,432			
5		$15,925				
6						
7						

Highlight cells B3, B4, C3, and C4. Do this by highlighting cell B3, and while still holding down the mouse button, drag down and to the right until all four cells are highlighted. Then hover over the lower right-hand corner of the highlighted cells until a crosshair or dot appears. It should look like this:

	A	B	C	D	E	F
1		January	February	March	April	May
2	Jennifer	$5,000	$5,050	$5,100	$5,150	$5,200
3	Curtis	$5,500	$5,400			
4	Kara	$5,425	$5,432			
5		$15,925				
6						

Grab the crosshair or dot and drag to the right until reaching column G, then let go. This will be the result:

	A	B	C	D	E	F
1		January	February	March	April	May
2	Jennifer	$5,000	$5,050	$5,100	$5,150	$5,200
3	Curtis	$5,500	$5,400	$5,300	$5,200	$5,100
4	Kara	$5,425	$5,432	$5,439	$5,446	$5,453
5		$15,925				
6						

As you can see, the spreadsheet automatically continued the series in each row. In Curtis' case, his earnings dropped $100 per month, while Kara's rose $7 per month.

Dragging to extend functions

There's one last trick to show with AutoFill. Cell B5 doesn't contain a typed value or a value that is part of a series. Instead, the number in cell B5 was generated by a formula. If you highlight it and look in the Formula Bar, you'll see "=SUM(B2:B4)". As you may remember from Chapter 1, SUM adds the amounts in the cells that are listed inside the parentheses (in this case, the range of cells from B2 to B4). What happens when that formula gets dragged across the screen?

Let's take a look. Highlight cell B5, hover your mouse over the lower right corner of the cell, and drag to the right until you reach column G. Let go of the mouse. This is what you should see:

B5		× ✓ *fx*	=SUM(B2:B4)			
	A	**B**	**C**	**D**	**E**	**F**
1		January	February	March	April	May
2	Jennifer	$5,000	$5,050	$5,100	$5,150	$5,200
3	Curtis	$5,500	$5,400	$5,300	$5,200	$5,100
4	Kara	$5,425	$5,432	$5,439	$5,446	$5,453
5		$15,925	$15,882	$15,839	$15,796	$15,753
6						
7						

When a formula is dragged across columns, it performs the same function for the designated cells in each column. It will also preserve the formatting. Select cell C5, and the Formula Bar will show =SUM(C2:C4). The amount is $15,882, which is the sum of cells C2, C3, and C4. Select cell D5, and the sum of cells D2 to D4 are shown.

What if you kept on dragging to cell H5? Try it. The cell will show "$0". Why? Because it's adding cells H2, H3, and H4, which are blank.

If you have tried to create this spreadsheet on your own and are having trouble, visit the book's official website at *excel.in30minutes.com*. You'll find an Excel version that you can download, as well as a Google Sheets version that you can manipulate right in your browser.

CHAPTER 2

More basic Excel skills: percentages, pasting, and rows

Over the past 10 minutes you have learned some of the basics of Excel, including addition, text formatting, and functions. You also have learned your first spreadsheet ninja skill—AutoFill—and have seen how it can save time. In the next five minutes, we'll work with multiplication, percentages, formatting numbers, and adding extra rows and columns. You'll also learn a few tricks with cells and worksheets.

For this chapter, we'll return to the earnings of our three chums in sales. Make sure that you've saved the results from the last chapter. If the spreadsheet file that we've been working on is not handy, go to the book website (*excel.in30minutes.com*), where you'll find the Excel and Google Spreadsheets versions of the file. You can also just follow along, using the screen images provided in the book.

Working with multiple worksheets

The data that you created in Chapter 1—the projected earnings of Jennifer, Curtis, and Kara from January to June—are going to be copied over to a new worksheet in the same spreadsheet file.

Wait a second. Why use another worksheet? Why not simply create a new copy of the spreadsheet file?

Spreadsheet programs have a useful feature that lets users "stack" worksheets inside a single file. It's very useful for organizing data in a single file. For instance, if you are working with annual financial data, you can put 2016 data on the top worksheet, 2017 data on the second worksheet, and the results for 2018 below that. It's also possible to link data on different worksheets, as we'll see later in this chapter.

How to create a new worksheet

Let's create the new worksheet in our Monthly Earnings spreadsheet file. (If you see Sheet1, Sheet2, and Sheet3 already located at the bottom of the worksheet, you can skip this step).

To create a second worksheet, go to the bottom of the existing worksheet. You'll see it's called Sheet1:

	A	B	C	D	E	F
1		January	February	March	April	May
2	Jennifer	$5,000	$5,050	$5,100	$5,150	$5,200
3	Curtis	$5,500	$5,400	$5,300	$5,200	$5,100
4	Kara	$5,425	$5,432	$5,439	$5,446	$5,453
5		$15,925	$15,882	$15,839	$15,796	$15,753
6						
7						

Click the plus symbol ("+") next to Sheet1. If not, right-click on the Sheet1 tab, select *Insert*, and then pick the *Worksheet* option.

The spreadsheet program will instantly create a new blank worksheet called Sheet2:

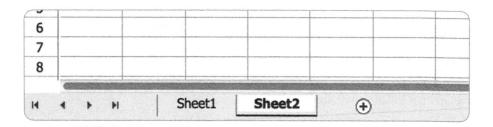

You can rearrange the sheets by selecting and dragging them to the right or left.

Copy, paste, and paste special

The next step is to copy the data from Sheet1 to Sheet2. To view the earnings data in Sheet1, simply select the Sheet1 tab. Select all of the cells that contain data by highlighting the top left cell (A1) and moving the mouse down and to the right until you reach cell G5. Copy the data by choosing *Edit > Copy* from the menu. Or, hover your mouse over the highlighted data, right-click and select *Copy* from the menu that appears.

Next, select the Sheet2 tab, using the tab at the bottom of the page. All of the cells will be empty, but cell A1 of Sheet2 will be selected by default. We're going to paste the data from Sheet1 in Sheet2. We'll use the same method that is commonly used in other programs, such as Microsoft Word or an email program.

In Excel, select the *Paste* button in the Home ribbon, and then choose the first small icon labelled paste. For Google Sheets, choose *Edit > Paste* from the menu, or right-click and select *Paste* from the menu that appears:

While copying and pasting is a straightforward process, there are some additional considerations. A cell can contain visible data, such as numbers or text. A cell may also contain a formula or have special formatting. Microsoft Excel, Excel Online, and Google Sheets all have options to paste only the raw values, or formulae and formatting information.

For our exercise, we have to make sure that formatting, formulas, and values were pasted into Sheet2. To confirm, follow these steps:

➤ **Values:** Do the numbers match up on each sheet (for example, is the value in Sheet1, cell B2 the same as the value in Sheet2, cell B2)?

➤ **Formatting:** Are the column headers on Sheet2 formatted in the same way as those on Sheet2?

➤ **Formulas:** Select cell B5 in Sheet1 and look in the Formula Bar. You'll see it contains the function "=SUM(B2:B4)". In Sheet2, does the Formula Bar display the same formula when you select cell B5?

If you answered "No" to any of these questions, you'll need to re-paste the data into Sheet2 using Paste Special.

Here's how to do it in Excel:

1. Clear the data in Sheet2 so that all of the cells are blank.

2. Return to Sheet1, and copy all of the data.

3. Go back to Sheet2, and select cell A1.

4. Select the *Paste* button in the Home ribbon to view a drop-down containing many paste options.

5. As you hover in the drop-down, a small tooltip will indicate the purpose of the option. For now, choose *Paste Special.*

After clicking in the drop-down, the following pop-up window will appear:

"All" is selected by default, which is what we want.

Select *OK,* and the contents, formulas, formatting, and even column widths will be pasted over to Sheet2.

How to duplicate a worksheet

There is a shortcut to copy all of the information (including formulas and formatting) from one worksheet to another: Simply duplicate the worksheet. Here's how:

➤ **Excel:** Right-click on the tab and select *Move Or Copy*. Highlight the worksheet you want to copy and select the checkbox that says *Create A Copy*.

➤ **Google Sheets:** Activate the small arrow on the Sheet1 tab and then select *Duplicate*.

➤ **Excel Online** can add blank worksheets to a spreadsheet file, but cannot currently duplicate an existing worksheet.

Adding rows

We're going to leave Sheet1 alone for now and work on Sheet2.

On Sheet2, we're going to project the earnings of the three friends over the next several months. We'll keep the original data that we copied over from Sheet1, but let's create three additional rows below each of the names on Sheet2. Two of the rows will contain values, while the third row is blank (this makes Sheet2 a little easier to understand).

In Excel or Excel Online, select the cell containing "Curtis" and click the *Insert* button in the Home ribbon. In the drop-down that appears, select *Insert Sheet Rows*. In Google Sheets, select *Insert > Row above* from the menu. A new row will appear above his name. Repeat this action to create two more rows between Jennifer and Curtis.

Then, create three empty rows below Curtis, and three empty rows below Kara. The result should look like this:

	A	B	C	D	E
1		January	February	March	April
2	Jennifer	$5,000	$5,050	$5,100	$5
3					
4					
5					
6	Curtis	$5,500	$5,400	$5,300	$5
7					
8					
9					
10	Kara	$5,425	$5,432	$5,439	$5
11					
12					
13					
14		$15,925	$15,882	$15,839	$15

What happens to functions, formulas, and references

The function to calculate the total earnings for January added up the amounts in cells B2, B3, and B4, and displayed the results in cell B5 (see Sheet1). However, on Sheet2, cells B3, B4, and B5 are now empty. Curtis' and Kara's monthly earnings from January are now located in cells B6 and B10, respectively. Yet the correct total for the month of January is still shown in B14. How can the function still work, if the cells have moved around?

Spreadsheet programs such as Microsoft Excel and Google Sheets are generally very forgiving when users move things around a worksheet. In most circumstances, Functions and values automatically update when you move a range of values and functions, or add rows and columns. For Sheet2, the functions and values reflect the new rows that were added.

Using percentages

Now, we're going to make another set of predictions for each person on the team. Let's start with Jennifer.

Under the original prediction, her earnings rise $50 per month. Let's calculate how her earnings rise at a rate of 1% per month:

1. In cell A3, type "Alternate rate (Jennifer)".

2. In cell A3, type "Alternate earnings (Jennifer)".

If the text in cells A2 or A3 is cut off, move the column divider between columns A and B to the right, as described in "Your first spreadsheet formula" in Chapter 1.

Because the growth starts in February, type ".01" in cell C3:

⊿	A	B	C	
1		**January**	**February**	**M**
2	Jennifer	$5,000	$5,050	
3	Alternate rate (Jennifer)		0.01	
4	Alternate earnings (Jennifer)			
5				
6	Curtis	$5,500	$5,400	

If you see $0.01, $0, 0, or something else besides "0.01", it means cell C3 has been formatted to hold currency values or some other number format. Continue to follow the instructions below to reformat the numbers—you'll still end up with the same result.

".01" is simply another way of saying "1%". However, for most people, it's easier to understand if the data is displayed as a percentage. To do this in Excel or Excel Online, highlight the cell, and activate the % button in the Home ribbon. Alternately, activate the small arrow for the Number Format dropdown menu on the Home ribbon. In Excel, you will see something like this:

Select *Percentage*, set *Decimal Places* to 0, and select *OK*.

To get the same result in Google Sheets, click the % button on the toolbar or choose *Format > Number > Percent* from the menu.

	B	C	D	
	January	**February**	**March**	**Apr**
	$5,000	$5,050	$5,100	$
ifer)		1%		
Jennifer)				

We want to show what happens when Jennifer's earnings rise 1% per month compared to $50 per month, using the same starting amount for January. The results for February will therefore reflect January earnings + 1%.

Since we're starting with the same figure in both scenarios, type "=B2" in cell B4. This tells the worksheet to display whatever is in cell B2 in cell B4. This is the result:

	A	B	C
1		**January**	**February**	**M**
2	Jennifer	$5,000	$5,050	
3	Alternate rate (Jennifer)		1%	
4	Alternate earnings (Jennifer)	$5,000		
5				
6	Curtis	$5,500	$5,400	

Some older versions of Excel may not automatically apply the dollar format to cell B4. If B4 appears as a real number, you'll need to reformat it for currencies/no decimal places using the instructions given earlier. While you're at it, do the same for all cells from C4 to G4, as they will all contain dollar values.

Why not manually type "$5000" in cell B4? The answer: Doing so may require you to change it again later. For instance, you may change Jennifer's starting earnings for January. By placing "=B2" in cell B4, you would only need to make the change in one location (B2), and it automatically carries over to the other cell (B4).

Now, select C4. This is where the alternate earnings for February, based on Jennifer's 1% increase from the previous month, will appear. Type ="B4*C3" here:

	A	B	C	
1		January	February	M
2	Jennifer	$5,000	$5,050	
3	Alternate rate (Jennifer)		1%	
4	Alternate earnings (Jennifer)	$5,000	=B4*C3	
5				
6	Curtis	$5,500	$5,400	

This tells the spreadsheet to multiply the value in B4 ($5000) by the value in C3 (1%) and show the result.

However, an unexpected result appears:

	A	B	C	
1		January	February	M
2	Jennifer	$5,000	$5,050	
3	Alternate rate (Jennifer)		1%	
4	Alternate earnings (Jennifer)	$5,000	$50	
5				
6				

Why is the result only $50? It's a simple mistake. If you multiply $5,000 by 1%, the result is 1% of $5,000, which is $50. We want to *add* that amount to Jennifer's January earnings—in other words, add 100% (the previous month's total) and 1% (the increase). How can this be done?

There are multiple ways to tackle this problem. Drop any of the following formulas into cell C4, and you will get the same result. Note that the asterisk symbol is used for multiplication:

=B4*1.01

=B4*101%

=B4+(B4*C3)

=B4*(1+C3)

Let's use the last option. It's important to include a reference to cell C3 in the formula. It saves a lot of work if we decide to use another percentage (for instance, 2%) later on—all we have to do is change the percentage value in cell C3, and cell C4 will automatically update.

Parentheses and PEMDAS

Let's take a closer look at the recommended formula:

=B4*(1+C3)

If we input the values from our worksheet, this represents $5,000 x (1+.01). Why are parentheses necessary? It's because Excel, Google Sheets, and other spreadsheet programs use the standard mathematical order of operations to determine what to do first. The order is Parentheses, Exponents, Multiplication, Division, Addition, and Subtraction, or PEMDAS (commonly remembered by the phrase "Please Excuse My Dear Aunt Sally").

Consider what would happen if we didn't use parentheses:

=B4*1+C3

The spreadsheet program would first multiply B4 ($5,000) by 1 and then add C3 (1%, or .01). This generates a result of $5,000.01. This is *not* what we want.

Parentheses force Excel to perform the addition first. This generates "101%" and multiplies it by the contents of cell B4 (that is, $5,000 times 101%).

Entering "=B4*(1+C3)" in cell C4 generates the following result:

◢	A	B	C	
1		**January**	**February**	**M**
2	Jennifer	$5,000	$5,050	
3	Alternate rate (Jennifer)		1%	
4	Alternate earnings (Jennifer)	$5,000	$5,050	
5				
6	Curtis	$5,500	$5,400	

What happens when the 1% growth rate is applied from March to June? The AutoFill method described in Excel Ninja Skill #1 can also be used to replicate the formula we just entered into cell C4 across all of the remaining months.

Because the formula depends on the percentage in row 3, we have to place values in the empty cells that will be referenced by the formula. Dragging a single value will copy that value to subsequent columns. Let's do that for cell B4—drag it across to column H. This is what you should see:

1		January	February	March	April	May
2	Jennifer	$5,000	$5,050	$5,100	$5,150	$5,200
3	Alternate rate (Jennifer)		1%	1%	1%	1%
4	Alternate earnings (Jennifer)	$5,000	$5,050			
5						
6	Curtis	$5,500	$5,400	$5,300	$5,200	$5,100
7						
8						

Now let's drag the formula in row 4, so we can see how 1% monthly growth affects Jennifer's earnings. Select cell C4, and hover over the dot in the lower right corner until a crosshair appears. Then drag it to the right until column G (June) is reached. Release the mouse. This is the result:

1		January	February	March	April	May
2	Jennifer	$5,000	$5,050	$5,100	$5,150	$5,200
3	Alternate rate (Jennifer)		1%	1%	1%	1%
4	Alternate earnings (Jennifer)	$5,000	$5,050	$5,101	$5,152	$5,203
5						
6	Curtis	$5,500	$5,400	$5,300	$5,200	$5,100
7						
8						

If you select any cell between B4 and G4 and look in the Formula Bar, you will see that it takes the earnings from the previous month, and multiplies that number by 101%. This is the same as 1% monthly growth.

In the long run, which scenario is better for Jennifer: an additional $50 per month, or 1% monthly growth? The answer can be determined by comparing the two earnings scenarios.

You can experiment with the growth rate in row 3. Change a few cells to different values (for example, 1% in February, 2% in March, 1% in April, 2% in May, 3% in June), or change everything. This will change the alternate earnings totals for all the months. For instance, if you change all of the values from 1% to 3%, this is what Jennifer gets:

◢	A	B	C	D	E	F
1		**January**	**February**	**March**	**April**	**May**
2	Jennifer	$5,000	$5,050	$5,100	$5,150	$5,200
3	Alternate rate (Jennifer)		3%	3%	3%	3%
4	Alternate earnings (Jennifer)	$5,000	$5,150	$5,305	$5,464	$5,628
5						
6	Curtis	$5,500	$5,400	$5,300	$5,200	$5,100

What a difference a few percentage points make!

Next, we'll create alternate earnings projections for the other two people on the team.

Declining percentages

Let's start with Curtis. Add "Alternate rate (Curtis)" and "Alternate earnings (Curtis)" to the cells below his name. While we're at it, let's do the same for Kara.

Curtis' original scenario was a decrease of $100 per month. Let's set it up so the decrease is 2% per month.

1. In cell C7, type "-2%", and drag that value across the row to column G (June).

2. Since we are starting at the same dollar amount in January for both methods, select cell B8 and type "=B6":

◢	A	B	C	D	E	F
1		**January**	**February**	**March**	**April**	**May**
2	Jennifer	$5,000	$5,050	$5,100	$5,150	$5,200
3	Alternate rate (Jennifer)		3%	3%	3%	3%
4	Alternate earnings (Jennifer)	$5,000	$5,150	$5,305	$5,464	$5,628
5						
6	Curtis	$5,500	$5,400	$5,300	$5,200	$5,100
7	Alternate rate (Curtis)		-2%	-2%	-2%	-2%
8	Alternate earnings (Curtis)	=B6				

This is the same way we matched up Jennifer's starting points. Press *Return/ Enter*, and this is the result:

	A	B	C	D	E	F
1		**January**	**February**	**March**	**April**	**May**
2	Jennifer	$5,000	$5,050	$5,100	$5,150	$5,200
3	Alternate rate (Jennifer)		3%	3%	3%	3%
4	Alternate earnings (Jennifer)	$5,000	$5,150	$5,305	$5,464	$5,628
5						
6	Curtis	$5,500	$5,400	$5,300	$5,200	$5,100
7	Alternate rate (Curtis)		-2%	-2%	-2%	-2%
8	Alternate earnings (Curtis)	$5,500				
9						
10	Kara	$5,425	$5,432	$5,439	$5,446	$5,453

What formula shall we enter into cell C8 to calculate Curtis' alternate earnings for February? For Jennifer, it was this:

$$\text{January Amount} * (1 + \text{rate})$$

Because we have set up Curtis' earnings to decrease each month, it should be something like the following, right?

$$\text{January Amount} * (1 - \text{rate})$$

Not so fast! Curtis' rate was entered as a *negative* percentage. If you subtract a negative, the result is positive, and each of the cells for the Alternate Rate would instead show an *increase* for Curtis.

Instead, all we need to do is use the same basic formula as we did for Jennifer, modified for the values in Curtis' rows. It's adding the –2% to 100% (1), which equals 98%. So, we enter the following into cell C8:

	A	B	C	D	E	F
1		**January**	**February**	**March**	**April**	**May**
2	Jennifer	$5,000	$5,050	$5,100	$5,150	$5,200
3	Alternate rate (Jennifer)		3%	3%	3%	3%
4	Alternate earnings (Jennifer)	$5,000	$5,150	$5,305	$5,464	$5,628
5						
6	Curtis	$5,500	$5,400	$5,300	$5,200	$5,100
7	Alternate rate (Curtis)		-2%	-2%	-2%	-2%
8	Alternate earnings (Curtis)	$5,500	=B8*(1+C7)		$5,200	$5,100

Once the result shows in cell C8, drag the formula across the remaining months, to June. You should see this:

⊿	A	B	C	D	E	F
1		January	February	March	April	May
2	Jennifer	$5,000	$5,050	$5,100	$5,150	$5,200
3	Alternate rate (Jennifer)		3%	3%	3%	3%
4	Alternate earnings (Jennifer)	$5,000	$5,150	$5,305	$5,464	$5,628
5						
6	Curtis	$5,500	$5,400	$5,300	$5,200	$5,100
7	Alternate rate (Curtis)		-2%	-2%	-2%	-2%
8	Alternate earnings (Curtis)	$5,500	$5,390	$5,282	$5,177	$5,073

A constant monthly decrease of 2% looks a little worse than a $100 monthly decrease. However, if the 2% decrease continues (and Curtis doesn't get fired), the 2% monthly decline will drop to less than $100 in the late summer. You can see for yourself by dragging the results beyond column G.

Static cell references

If you know that Curtis' monthly decline will remain constant at 2%, why is it even necessary to have a whole row of cells that say the same thing ("-2%")? Wouldn't it be easier to simply enter the figure once, and then refer to the same cell each month?

Indeed it would! Here's how to do it, using *dollar signs* appended to the cell reference:

1. Clear "-2%" from all cells in the row except for cell C7.
2. Clear rows D8 through G8.
3. Select cell C8. The formula bar should display "=B8*(1+C7)".
4. Change the formula to "=B8*(1+$C$7)" and press *Return/Enter*. The result in C8 is the same as it was before.
5. Drag the cell's formula across the remaining months, until cell G8, and release the mouse.

The result in cells D8 through G8 are the same as before.

Changing the formula to reference $C$7 tells the spreadsheet to always refer to that cell, even when the formula is dragged to later months. Select cells D8 through G8 and look at the formulas in the Formula Bar. You'll see that only the references to the previous month's earnings change from month to month, while the rate value is always taken from the same cell—C7. For example, Curtis' alternate earnings for June were originally based on this formula, in which F8 contained the earnings for May, and G7 was the rate for June:

$$=F8*(1+G7)$$

Now, the growth rate references the same cell as all of the other months:

$$=F8*(1+$C$7)$$

Spreadsheet division

Kara's monthly earnings, shown on row 10 in Sheet2, were originally projected to increase $7 per month. But Kara has decided she wants to transition to a new part-time role, and eventually leave the company in order to get her singing career off the ground. What will happen if her earnings are cut in half every month?

It's possible to follow the same model as Curtis, and use a rate that reflects a monthly decline of 50%. Or, simply multiply the previous month's earnings by 50%.

Let's try another method: division. Kara's earnings are divided in half every month, or:

$$Earnings/2$$

For February, it's possible to write this as a simple formula:

$$=B12/2$$

where B12 is the same earnings starting point for January ("=B10") and 2 is the denominator. Then, you can drag out the formula to June using AutoFill.

However, there are two problems with this approach:

1. You can't see what the formula is based on, simply by looking at the cells.

2. If you decide to change the denominator, it would require redoing the formulas from February to June.

Let's use a reference to a fixed value instead, just like we did for Curtis. Change the label for row 11 to "Alternate denominator (Kara)." First, enter "=B2" into cell B12. Then, in cell C11, type the number 2. If it displays as a dollar amount or percentage, go to the Number Format drop-down menu on the Home ribbon (Excel) or *Format > Number* (Google Sheets) and change it to a number.

In cell C12, type this:

6	Curtis	$5,500	$5,400
7	Alternate rate (Curtis)		-2%
8	Alternate earnings (Curtis)	$5,500	$5,390
9			
10	Kara	$5,425	$5,432
11	Alternate rate (Kara)		2
12	Alternate earnings (Kara)	$5,425	=B12/$C$11

This shows the result for February, based on dividing the January earnings for Kara by 2:

6	Curtis	$5,500	$5,400
7	Alternate rate (Curtis)		-2%
8	Alternate earnings (Curtis)	$5,500	$5,390
9			
10	Kara	$5,425	$5,432
11	Alternate rate (Kara)		2
12	Alternate earnings (Kara)	$5,425	$2,713

Now, drag the formula from cell C12 (February) to G12 (June):

6	Curtis	$5,500	$5,400	$5,300	$5,200	$5,100
7	Alternate rate (Curtis)		-2%			
8	Alternate earnings (Curtis)	$5,500	$5,390	$5,282	$5,177	$5,073
9						
10	Kara	$5,425	$5,432	$5,439	$5,446	$5,453
11	Alternate rate (Kara)		2			
12	Alternate earnings (Kara)	$5,425	$2,713	$1,356	$678	$339

By April, Kara's earnings have dropped below $1,000, and by June, they're only a little over $150.

Referencing other worksheets

There's a problem with Sheet1. Look at the bottom row (row 14), which shows total monthly earnings for all three employees:

8	Alternate earnings (Curtis)	$5,500	$5,390	$5,282	$5,177	$5,073
9						
10	Kara	$5,425	$5,432	$5,439	$5,446	$5,453
11	Alternate rate (Kara)		2			
12	Alternate earnings (Kara)	$5,425	$2,713	$1,356	$678	$339
13						
14		$26,425	$26,424	$26,426	$26,436	$26,454

Considering Kara's earnings have dropped so sharply, why is the total little changed from January to June?

The answer: The total earnings were calculated using AutoSum or SUM on a range of cells. When we added the extra rows between the three names, the range expanded to include the new rows. Then, when we added the alternate earnings for each person, those values were added to the combined monthly total as well.

Go back to Sheet1. Cell F5 contains the following formula

$$=SUM(F2: F4)$$

This formula adds the contents of just three cells: the monthly earnings for Jennifer (F2), Curtis (F3), and Kara (F4):

F5			=SUM(F2:F4)				
	A	B	C	D	E	F	
1		January	February	March	April	May	
2	Jennifer	$5,000	$5,050	$5,100	$5,150	$5,200	
3	Curtis	$5,500	$5,400	$5,300	$5,200	$5,100	
4	Kara	$5,425	$5,432	$5,439	$5,446	$5,453	
5		$15,925	$15,882	$15,839	$15,796	$15,753	

Take a look at the same column in Sheet2. Cell F14 contains the formula "=SUM(F2:F10)", which means all of the cells from F2 to F10 are included in the total. That needs to be fixed. There should be two totals for each month: one showing the original total for the three workers, and the other showing the alternate earnings total for the group. Here's how to set it up:

1. On Sheet2, clear the values in row 14.

2. In cell A14, create a new label: "Original total".

3. In the cell below it, create another label: "Alternate total".

For the original monthly totals, we could enter a new formula that adds together the original earnings for each worker. But why do that, when the data is already available on Sheet1?

Yes, it's possible to reference cells on another worksheet. This is not only a timesaver, but it also makes it possible to change a value in one location and have those changes carry over to other cells and sheets that reference it. Here's how to do it, using Excel, Excel Online, or Google Sheets:

1. Go to Sheet1, and determine which cell contains the original total for January (it should be B5)

2. Go to Sheet2. In cell B14, type this:

=Sheet1!B5

Assuming the formula was entered correctly, you should see this:

8	Alternate earnings (Curtis)	$5,500	$5,390	$5,282	$5,177	$5,073
9						
10	Kara	$5,425	$5,432	$5,439	$5,446	$5,453
11	Alternate rate (Kara)		$2			
12	Alternate earnings (Kara)	$5,425	$2,713	$1,356	$678	$339
13						
14	Original total	$15,925				
15	Alternate total					

Dragging the formula across to May, the original total is shown for each month.

Using the name of the sheet followed by an exclamation point and the cell reference tells the spreadsheet to use the value in the cell on the named sheet. Keep in mind that if you make a mistake or reference the wrong worksheet, you'll get an error message ("#REF!").

Finally, let's add up the alternate amounts for each month. This can be done simply by adding up the values in the Alternate Earnings cells in column B, as we show in the figure:

4	Alternate earnings (Jennifer)	$5,000	$5,150	$5,305	$5,464	$5,628
5						
6	Curtis	$5,500	$5,400	$5,300	$5,200	$5,100
7	Alternate rate (Curtis)		-2%	-2%	-2%	-2%
8	Alternate earnings (Curtis)	$5,500	$5,390	$5,282	$5,177	$5,073
9						
10	Kara	$5,425	$5,432	$5,439	$5,446	$5,453
11	Alternate rate (Kara)		$2			
12	Alternate earnings (Kara)	$5,425	$2,713	$1,356	$678	$339
13						
14	Original total	$15,925				
15	Alternate total	=B4+B8+B12				

Use AutoFill to drag the formula across the remaining months. Your table is complete (for now):

10	Kara	$5,425	$5,432	$5,439	$5,446	$5,453
11	Alternate rate (Kara)		$2			
12	Alternate earnings (Kara)	$5,425	$2,713	$1,356	$678	$339
13						
14	Original total	$15,925	$15,882	$15,839	$15,796	$15,753
15	Alternate total	$15,925	$13,253	$11,943	$11,318	$11,040

By now, you've learned how to use multiplication and division, how to use percentages to calculate growth rates, how to reference fixed cells in formulas, and how to reference cells in another worksheet. Next, we'll learn another ninja skill—charts.

Chapter quiz

1. Show the formula to multiply 1023 by 9.12.

2. How would .05 be converted to a percentage?

3. You inherit $10,000 at the beginning of 2017 and decide to invest it all in a five-year certificate of deposit that bears 5% interest (compounded annually). What will the balance be when the term ends in early 2022?

4. In a new worksheet, create a list of four family members or friends and their approximate weight in pounds or kilograms. How could you quickly convert the weights from one system to the other? (1 kilogram=2.2 pounds).

Answers can be found in Appendix II on page 94.

Excel Ninja skill #2: charts

If AutoFill is the Japanese throwing star of spreadsheets, then making charts surely is the equivalent of Japanese calligraphy. With just a few clicks of the mouse, it's possible to turn your raw data into visual presentations that will impress all who come near.

Chart wizards

Charts are one of the most effective ways to communicate data and trends. At one time, they were difficult to make, requiring design skills and/or special tools. Nowadays, anyone can make great-looking charts using Microsoft Excel or Google Sheets. It's not hard to do—both programs contain standard templates for pie charts, line charts, scatter plots, and more. While Excel's chart formatting options are powerful, charts created with Google Sheets look great and are easier to manipulate. It's possible to create simple charts with Excel Online, but customization is limited.

As we only have 15 minutes left, we'll create a simple pie chart. But once you've learned how to do one chart, it's not hard to figure out how to create another type, such as a bar chart or line chart. As long as the right kind of data is selected, the steps to make any type of chart are almost identical. In addition, you'll learn how to make basic customizations in both Excel and Google Sheets.

We'll be using the data from the earlier exercises with Jennifer, Curtis, and Kara to make charts. If you don't have it available, you can use the Excel and Google Sheets versions on the book's official website (*excel.in30minutes. com*; look for "Sample Spreadsheets").

Pie charts

In the Monthly Earnings file, go to Sheet1. As you recall, this contains the original monthly earnings projections for our three friends. We're going to make a simple pie chart, based on their monthly earnings for January.

On Sheet1, select cell A1, and then drag down to cell B4. Eight cells will be selected in all:

	A	B	C	D	A
1		**January**	**February**	**March**	A
2	**Jennifer**	$5,000	$5,050	$5,100	$
3	**Curtis**	$5,500	$5,400	$5,300	$
4	**Kara**	$5,425	$5,432	$5,439	$
5		$15,925	$15,882	$15,839	$
6					
7					
8					

It's important to include the names of the people and the month. The spreadsheet program will use the selected text for the labels inside of the pie chart, and will determine the numerical values to use in the chart.

To make the chart in Excel, go to the Insert ribbon and select the button that looks like a tiny pie chart. The following options will be displayed:

Google Sheets has a similar button:

Pressing it brings up the Chart Editor:

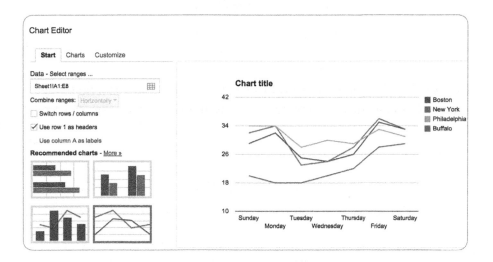

If the button is not visible, go to *Insert > Chart.* The wizard will appear.

Regardless of which program is used, the chart wizards work in the same way: Select the data, choose the chart type, and the chart will be placed right on the worksheet. The chart can then be moved around, edited, or reformatted.

Here's what appears in Excel, after creating a two-dimensional pie chart based on the January earnings on Sheet1:

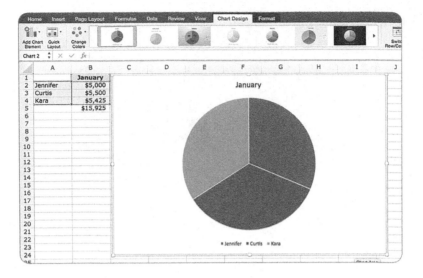

Not bad for 10 seconds of work! Once created, the chart can be dragged around the page or exported as an image file (see "Exporting charts" in Chapter 4).

Customizing charts

The pie chart can also be improved. Here are some elements that could be changed:

➤ **Chart title:** It's currently based on the column header, but "January Earnings" is clearer.

➤ **Missing labels:** There are no labels on the pie sections.

The following section explains how to make these changes.

Editing charts in Excel

There are three ways to make changes to charts in recent versions of Microsoft Excel:

1. Select the cookie-cutter styles under Chart Tools or the Chart Design ribbon which appears when working with charts.

2. Change options by selecting *Add Chart Element, Quick Layout, Change Colors* and *Change Chart Type* buttons on the Chart Design ribbon.

3. Select individual elements on the chart to edit text or make other changes.

4. Right-click over individual elements to select other options (this may be the only option available in older versions of Excel).

The variations shown in the cookie-cutter options as well as under the *Quick Layout* button are the easiest to apply. Here are the options for the layout of the pie chart:

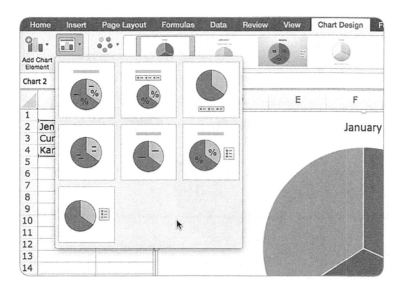

Double-clicking or right-clicking the colored chart elements in Excel will display the *Format Data Series* or *Format Data Point* options. You will be presented with sophisticated chart formatting options, but these are only available to users of the desktop version (Excel Online and Google Sheets are much more limited when it comes to formatting charts). In addition, while changing the fill color, expanding the size of the line surrounding the legend, applying 3D elements, and tweaking gradients and drop-shadows are all nice-to-have options in Excel, they are unnecessary for most projects.

There is still one more edit to make to the pie chart: Change the title from "January" to "January Earnings." To do this, simply select the title and input the change.

Editing charts in Google Sheets

Google Sheets has an easier interface for making and editing charts. For instance, the chart labels that have to be manually set up in some versions of Microsoft Excel are activated by default in Google Sheets.

Editing is very simple. Click the chart once, and a banner appears. This is Quick Edit mode. To see the options for a particular element, just click it once:

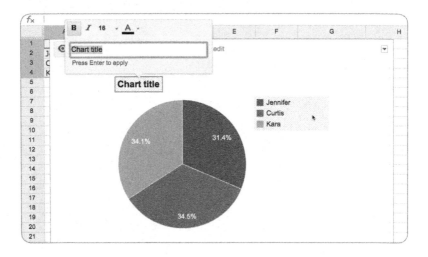

Column charts and line charts

Excel and Google Sheets also offer options for creating other kinds of charts:

➤ **Line charts** are used to show how a value changes over time, such as a stock market index or the price of gasoline.

➤ **Bar charts** use columns to compare values, and offer options such as grouping by time period and splitting columns into subsets. An example would be a chart that shows monthly revenue for a business, with the monthly total broken out into segments showing revenue from sales and revenue from services.

➤ **Scatter plots** show individual data points on an X/Y axis in order to highlight the relationships between the values on each axis. For instance, a scatter plot could be used to show the relationship between the math and science scores of a group of high school students.

Whatever chart type you pick, make sure the right data is selected before inserting a chart.

In certain situations, it may be possible to switch between chart types. However, the data must match the chart type. For instance, the pie chart we created in the last exercise (January Sales for Jennifer, Curtis, and Kara) would not be suitable for a line chart.

CHAPTER 3

Sorting and filtering

Have you ever seen a spreadsheet file with more than 1,000 rows of data, or more than 100 columns? It's not a pretty sight. However, if you begin using spreadsheet programs to track or manage marketplaces, websites, customer lists, school projects, geographic data, scientific experiments, and financial projections, you'll eventually have to deal with large sets of data.

This chapter will explain how to tame these massive beasts. Some of the techniques, such as hiding rows and columns, are mere organizational tools. But others—such as sorting and filtering—can help you make sense of large pools of data.

Excel not only has the most fine-grained sorting and filtering tools, it also can handle gigantic spreadsheets that can choke online spreadsheet programs such as Google Sheets and Excel Online. However, Google Sheets is adequate for all of the examples in this chapter. Excel Online currently offers basic sorting options, but no filtering tools.

Sorting

Think back to your primary school days, and those chaotic scenes in the gym or playground—teachers yelling at everyone in class to line up from the shortest to the tallest, the youngest to the oldest, or alphabetically by last name.

Sorting data in a spreadsheet follows a similar model. You're basically ordering the data by size, age, or value. If text is involved, it's being ordered alphabetically from A to Z—or in reverse, from Z to A.

Sorting can be used to manage large lists, but they can also bring order to smaller datasets. To illustrate, we'll be turning back to our three friends and their two earnings scenarios in the Monthly Earnings spreadsheets file.

We'll need to create a new worksheet with the data from Sheet2—but only the values and formats, not the formulas (sorting can break formulas, so it's better to work only with the values). Copy and paste the values and number formats onto a new sheet using the Paste Special methods described in Chapter 2.

Adjust the column widths and format the headers until you're left with something that looks like this:

	A	B	C	D	E	F	G
1		January	February	March	April	May	June
2	**Jennifer**	$5,000	$5,050	$5,100	$5,150	$5,200	$5,250
3	Alternate rate (Jennifer)		1%	1%	1%	1%	1%
4	Alternate earnings (Jennifer)	$5,000	$5,050	$5,101	$5,152	$5,203	$5,255
5							
6	**Curtis**	$5,500	$5,400	$5,300	$5,200	$5,100	$5,000
7	Alternate rate (Curtis)		-2%				
8	Alternate earnings (Curtis)	$5,500	$5,390	$5,282	$5,177	$5,073	$4,972
9							
10	**Kara**	$5,425	$5,432	$5,439	$5,446	$5,453	$5,460
11	Alternate denominator (Kara)		$2				
12	Alternate earnings (Kara)	$5,425	$2,713	$1,356	$678	$339	$170
13							

Hiding rows and columns

Next, we want to hide some of the data in the worksheet. We'll only be working with the rows containing original and alternate earnings projections for each person, so the following rows will be hidden:

➤ Alternate rates for Jennifer and Curtis, and the alternate denominator for Kara (however, alternate values for each person *will* be included).

➤ Original total.

➤ Alternate total.

➤ Blank rows.

Let's start with Jennifer's alternate rate. Right-click over the number 3 at the beginning of the row. On the menu that appears, select *Hide*. You can also use the *Format* button and drop-down menu on the Home ribbon, and select *Hide & Unhide > Hide Rows*. After doing so, you'll notice that row 3 appears to be missing—the row numbers jump from 2 to 4. But it hasn't been deleted. See for yourself:

1. Select rows 2 and 4 (by selecting the number 2 and dragging down to the number 4).

2. Right-click the two selected rows.

3. Select the *Unhide* option.

4. Row 3 will reappear.

Hide row 3 again, then do the same for the remaining rows that need to be hidden (refer to the list above). To hide the column for January, follow the same actions on the letter C above the column header for January's earnings.

At the end, you should be left with this:

	A	B	C	D	E	F	G
1		January	February	March	April	May	June
2	**Jennifer**	$5,000	$5,050	$5,100	$5,150	$5,200	$5,250
4	Alternate earnings (Jennifer)	$5,000	$5,050	$5,101	$5,152	$5,203	$5,255
6	**Curtis**	$5,500	$5,400	$5,300	$5,200	$5,100	$5,000
8	Alternate earnings (Curtis)	$5,500	$5,390	$5,282	$5,177	$5,073	$4,972
10	**Kara**	$5,425	$5,432	$5,439	$5,446	$5,453	$5,460
12	Alternate earnings (Kara)	$5,425	$2,713	$1,356	$678	$339	$170
13							

Rearranging a list in alphabetical order

Let's try the Sort feature. One of the most common use cases for sorting is rearranging a list in alphabetical order. For our short list, follow these steps:

Basic sorting in Excel

1. Select column A by clicking on the letter A above the names.

2. Press the *Sort & Filter* button in the Home ribbon.

3. Select the *Sort A-Z* option, if visible. If prompted, select Expand the selection. The entire list will be alphabetized.

4. If the *Sort A-Z* button is not visible in the Home ribbon, go to *the Data ribbon and* press the *A-Z* button.

5. Select *OK*. The list has been rearranged alphabetically (see below).

	A	B	C	D	E	F	G
1		January	February	March	April	May	June
2	Alternate earnings (Curtis)	$5,500	$5,390	$5,282	$5,177	$5,073	$4,972
4	Alternate earnings (Jennifer)	$5,000	$5,050	$5,101	$5,152	$5,203	$5,255
6	Alternate earnings (Kara)	$5,425	$2,713	$1,356	$678	$339	$170
8	**Curtis**	$5,500	$5,400	$5,300	$5,200	$5,100	$5,000
10	**Jennifer**	$5,000	$5,050	$5,100	$5,150	$5,200	$5,250
12	**Kara**	$5,425	$5,432	$5,439	$5,446	$5,453	$5,460
13							

There are a few things to note about what just happened:

➤ Excel sorted all of the columns so the results match up with the changes in column A.

➤ The headers in the other columns were not sorted.

➤ Why is it important to choose the *Expand the selection* option when prompted? If only one column is sorted, but the others are not, major problems can result. Consider a spreadsheet containing names and phone numbers, but only the names are sorted. Whoever uses the spreadsheet as a contact list will end up calling the wrong numbers.

➤ The data in the hidden rows was neither exposed nor was it sorted alphabetically. If you use the Unhide option, you will see that the hidden rows remained in the same positions before sorting.

➤ However, the hidden column (B, for January earnings) was sorted along with the other earnings columns. This is necessary to ensure that the January earnings line up with the other data that's being rearranged.

Basic sorting in Google Sheets

Sorting options in Google Sheets are accessed through the Data menu at the top of the browser window. Alphabetical sorting options are listed under

the menu, or you can select several columns to sort and then select *Data >
Sort Range*. This window looks different from its Excel counterpart, but it
basically has the same options and does the same thing:

An alternate sorting scenario

What if you wanted to sort the data so the results for June are arranged
from highest earnings to lowest? Here's how to do it:

1. Highlight the column containing June earnings.

2. Press the *Sort & Filter* button on the Home ribbon and select *Sort
   Largest to Smallest. Expand the selection* when prompted.

3. Alternately, select *Custom Sort*, or press the *Sort* button on the *Data*
   ribbon.

4. In the Sort window that appears, select the *Sort By* row and then
   select the drop-down menu under the *Column* header. Choose column G (June).

5. Under the *Order* drop-down, select *Largest to Smallest* and press *OK*.

This is the result:

	A	B	C	D	E	F	G
1		January	February	March	April	May	June
2	Kara	$5,425	$5,432	$5,439	$5,446	$5,453	$5,460
4	Alternate earnings (Jennifer)	$5,000	$5,050	$5,101	$5,152	$5,203	$5,255
6	Jennifer	$5,000	$5,050	$5,100	$5,150	$5,200	$5,250
8	Curtis	$5,500	$5,400	$5,300	$5,200	$5,100	$5,000
10	Alternate earnings (Curtis)	$5,500	$5,390	$5,282	$5,177	$5,073	$4,972
12	Alternate earnings (Kara)	$5,425	$2,713	$1,356	$678	$339	$170

Save this spreadsheet file on your hard drive or OneDrive, because we will be using Sheet3 to demonstrate Excel's filtering capabilities.

Sorting with multiple criteria

Another common scenario with sorting happens with worksheets that need to be sorted by more than one criteria.

For instance, a company's human resources department may have a spreadsheet that tracks holiday bonuses. The HR staff want to sort it alphabetically by department and then by amount, from highest to lowest.

If the names are listed in column A, the department in column B, and the amount for each employee in column C, then here's what the original spreadsheet would look like:

	A	B	C
1	Name	Department	Bonus
2	Eliza Lyons	Assembly	300
3	Sally Wang	Admin	250
4	Bill Kyne	Assembly	100
5	Mel Goldsmith	Assembly	125
6	Nathan Coca	Engineering	400
7	Terry Lawler	Engineering	1000
8	Beth Schultz	Engineering	700
9	Linda DiPerna	Admin	540
10	Jim Lawler	Transport	50
11	Ella Jones	Assembly	650

Here's how the list would be sorted in Excel:

1. Select all of the cells containing data by dragging from A1 to C11.

2. On the Home ribbon, press the *Sort & Filter* button and then *Custom Sort.* Alternately, go to the Data ribbon and press the *Sort* button.

3. In the Sort window (see screenshot, below), select the drop-down menu under *Column* and choose "Department." Under *Order,* choose *A to Z.*

4. Select the "+" button or *Add Level* to create a new row that will contain the "Then by" option.

5. Select the new row, and then select the column that contains the bonus amount (column C). Under *Order,* choose *Largest to Smallest.*

In Google Sheets, follow these steps:

1. Select all of the cells from A1 to C11.

2. Select *Data > Sort Range.* The Sort Range pop-up window will appear.

3. Select the *Data has header row* checkbox.

4. Change the *Sort By* drop-down to *Department* (Column B), and make sure *A to Z* is selected (this will make the list alphabetical by department).

5. Select the *Add another sort column* link. A new drop-down will appear. Change it to *Bonus,* and then select *Z to A* (this will order each amount from highest to lowest).

This is what you should see:

	A	B	C	D	E	F
1	Name	Department	Bonus			
2	Eliza Lyons	Assembly	$300			
3	Sally Wang	Admin	$250			
4	Bill Kyne	Assembly	$100			
5	Mel Goldsmith	Assembly	$125			
6	Nathan Coca	Engineering	$400			
7	Terry Lawler	Engineering	$1000			
8	Beth Schultz	Engineering	$700			
9	Linda DiPerna	Admin	$540			
10	Jim Lawler	Transport	$50			
11	Ella Jones	Assembly	$650			

Sort range from A1 to C11

☒ Data has header row

sort by   Department ⇕   ● A → Z   ○ Z → A

x then by   Bonus ⇕   ● A → Z   ○ Z → A

+ Add another sort column

[Sort]   Cancel

This is the result:

	A	B	C
1	**Name**	**Department**	**Bonus**
2	Linda DiPerna	Admin	540
3	Sally Wang	Admin	250
4	Ella Jones	Assembly	650
5	Eliza Lyons	Assembly	300
6	Mel Goldsmith	Assembly	125
7	Bill Kyne	Assembly	100
8	Terry Lawler	Engineering	1000
9	Beth Schultz	Engineering	700
10	Nathan Coca	Engineering	400
11	Jim Lawler	Transport	50

Setting up sorting for multiple criteria may seem confusing, but once you try it, you'll see it's actually quite easy. Visit the book's official website (*excel. in30minutes.com*) to see videos that show how to sort data using one or more criteria.

Filtering

Filtering is another way to highlight results in a long or complex list. The feature lets you display certain rows, while hiding everything else.

Here's a quick example in Excel, using Sheet3 from the Monthly Earnings spreadsheet.

Let's say we only wanted to display the June earnings in which someone made at least $5,000, and hide everything else:

1. Highlight column G ("June") by clicking on the letter "G" above cell G1.

2. In Excel, go to the Data ribbon and select the *Filter* button (or select *Sort & Filter > Filter* from the Home ribbon). In Google Sheets, select *Data > Filter.*

3. Look closely at column G. You will notice a tiny drop-down menu icon next to *June.* Select it.

In Excel, the following menu appears:

E	F	G	H	I	J
pril	May	June ▾			
$5,150	$5,200	$5,250	June		
$5,152	$5,203	$5,255	Sort		
$5,200	$5,100	$5,000	↕ Ascending ↕ Descending		
$5,177	$5,073	$4,972	By color: None		
$5,446	$5,453	$5,460	Filter		
$678	$339	$170	By color: None		
			Choos...		
			Q Search		
			☑ (Select All)		
			☑ $170		
			☑ $4,972		
			☑ $5,000		
			Clear Filter		

All of the values from June are listed in the menu. Select the checkbox next to "$5,000" and deselect everything else. Then press *OK*:

	A	B	C	D	E	F	G
1		January	February	March	April	May	June
8	Curtis	$5,500	$5,400	$5,300	$5,200	$5,100	$5,000
15							
16							
17							
18							

However, we want to include values that are greater than $5,000, too. Select the menu icon next to *June* and then access the drop-down menu that sets filtering rules. Select *Greater Than or Equal To* and type "5000" into the field next to it, and select *OK*. This is the result:

	A	B	C	D	E	F	G
1		January	February	March	April	May	June
2	Kara	$5,425	$5,432	$5,439	$5,446	$5,453	$5,460
4	Alternate earnings (Jennifer)	$5,000	$5,050	$5,101	$5,152	$5,203	$5,255
6	Jennifer	$5,000	$5,050	$5,100	$5,150	$5,200	$5,250
8	Curtis	$5,500	$5,400	$5,300	$5,200	$5,100	$5,000
14		$26,425	$26,324	$26,222	$26,124	$26,029	$25,937

Interesting. Now we have all of the rows for individuals that are equal to or greater than $5,000. A hidden row (row 14) may also be revealed, but this can be easily re-hidden using the directions given earlier in this chapter.

Google Sheets can also filter results using a similar interface accessed from *Data > Filter.* However, the options are more rudimentary—custom filters and rules are not available.

Nevertheless, it's easy to imagine how filters could be used to quickly isolate and order data from large lists. Examples include:

➤ Listing the highest-paid workers in a department with hundreds of employees.

➤ Identifying struggling students in a large high school.

➤ Tracking a transaction in a list of thousands of sales records, based on a specific amount.

If you're having trouble getting started with filters, there are some videos on the book's website (*excel.in30minutes.com*) that show you how to use them. There are also sample Google Sheets spreadsheets on the book website that you can copy and filter to your heart's content.

Only five more minutes to go! The last chapter explores what to do with your spreadsheet files once you've finished working on them. Get ready to try out printing, importing and exporting, and online sharing.

Chapter quiz

1. You have a list of students at the local high school that shows their first name (column A), last name (column B), ages (column C), and most recent math grade (expressed on a 100-point scale in column D). How would you order the list alphabetically by last name?

2. Using the same worksheet described in question #1, how would you display only the students who have failing grades in math? Assume that a failing grade is 60 or lower.

3. Why is it often necessary to expand the selection across multiple columns when using Sort?

Answers can be found in Appendix II on page 95.

CHAPTER 4

Printing, import/export features, and collaboration

We've covered a lot of ground in the past 25 minutes. Now it's time to get ready for the final act: getting your data out of the spreadsheet program and into whatever format is best for your masterpiece.

For most people, that will be a printed piece of paper. However, others share spreadsheets as PDFs that can be emailed or sent to someone else for printing. Another common scenario: exporting the data in a spreadsheet in a format that can be used by other programs.

Printing

Printing spreadsheets can be an exercise in frustration and wasted paper. While it's easy to print a worksheet (go to *File > Print* or select the *Print* button, if visible), the perspective is often wrong, and columns and headers can get cut off.

But there are ways of avoiding problems. Here are some tips for making printing go more smoothly:

Adjust column widths

You can manipulate column widths to squeeze more columns onto a single sheet of paper. However, this will also cause longer names or text phrases to break to more than one line, and may cause numbers to become unreadable (look for "######" in a cell, which indicates that the number is too long to fit into the width of a single cell). A better solution: Switch to landscape mode (described below).

Switch from portrait to landscape mode

If you've only printed out letters, tickets, emails, and Web pages in the past, you've probably been using *portrait* mode. This makes the text and other content fit onto a vertically oriented page. Spreadsheets printed out in portrait mode, which is the default for some versions of Microsoft Excel, can lead to cut-off columns.

Spreadsheets with lots of columns should be printed out in *landscape* mode. This flips the orientation, so the left-right axis is wider. To do this, follow these instructions:

Excel:

1. Go to *File > Page Setup*.

2. Select the *Landscape* option.

3. Optional: Change the *Fit To* settings under *Scaling* to fit more columns into a single page.

Google Sheets:

The default settings in Google Sheets are *Fit to width/Landscape* mode.

How to set the print area

This is a useful option for one-off print jobs, in which you have a giant spreadsheet but don't need to print all of the raw data. Instead, you only want to print out the summary or a small, critical area. Here's how to set up a print area:

Excel:

1. The default print area is marked with dashed blue lines to indicate the margins.

2. To set your own print area, select a group of cells and then select *File > Print Area > Set Print Area*.

3. To change margins, orientation, or other layout options, use the buttons on the Page Layout ribbon.

4. To clear the print area, select *File > Print Area > Clear Print Area*.

Excel Online:

➤ *File > Print* opens the print wizard with the option to print a selected group of cells or the entire sheet.

Google Sheets:

1. Select the cells you want to print.

2. Select *File > Print*. The Print Settings window will appear.

3. Under *Options*, choose *Selection*.

On some versions of Excel, a print area may already be set. Look for dashed horizontal and vertical lines on the spreadsheet, which are the guides that determine the edges of each printed page.

Printing cell outlines

While working on a spreadsheet, you'll see a grid that represents the borders between cells. When you print the document, the gridlines disappear. This makes the page look neater. However, for certain types of worksheets, you may want to include the gridlines on the printed page. To do this in Excel, follow these steps:

1. Go to the Page Layout ribbon.

2. Look for the small *Print* checkbox under *Gridlines*, and select it.

The gridlines will be included in the printed worksheet. Note that this option is currently unavailable in Excel Online (gridlines are off by default).

For Google Sheets, gridlines are the default option for printing, but these can be turned off by selecting the *No Gridlines* checkbox when you print a page.

Exporting PDFs

PDFs are a type of computer file that present text, graphics, and data almost exactly as it will appear on a printed page. You've probably received email attachments in PDF form, and may have seen PDFs in online search results.

When working with spreadsheets, PDFs offer a number of benefits:

1. PDFs are an easy way to send full-color spreadsheets to colleagues, clients, and service providers.

2. PDFs can be used to troubleshoot printing problems. Because PDFs give full-color, full-size representations of a worksheet on printed paper, they can be used to preview what your worksheet will look like when it is printed out. This is an excellent way to make sure that columns, graphics, and headers are showing up before you send the job to the printer.

3. If your printer is not working properly, you can save the file as a PDF and print it out somewhere else.

4. PDFs can't easily be edited by other people. This may be useful if you want to send a review copy of a spreadsheet to someone else, but don't want him or her to alter the values or formulas inside the file.

Here are the instructions for creating PDFs with various spreadsheet programs.

Excel for Windows

On Windows PCs, Excel 2003 and older versions of Microsoft's spreadsheet software do not support PDF creation out of the box. You'll have to buy additional software (for example, Adobe Acrobat or online PDF conversion software).

However, newer versions of Excel *do* support PDF creation. Go to *File > Save As*, and, using the *Save as type* drop-down menu, select PDF. On Excel 2016, you can also use *File > Export* and select *Create PDF/XPS document.*

Excel for Mac

1. In Excel, go to *File > Save As*. You can also select *File > Print*, which will bring up the Print window.

2. Select the *PDF* button or link in the pop-up window that appears.

3. Choose *Save As PDF*, or view the PDF in Preview, if you want to see what it looks like.

Excel Online

PDF exports are not possible with the current version of Excel Online. Depending on the computer you are using, you may be able to create a PDF by choosing *Save as PDF* when selecting a printer.

Google Sheets:

➤ Go to *File > Download As > PDF.*

Importing and exporting

We've covered printing and how to save worksheets as PDF files. Now it's time to discuss how to import files into Excel, and the process of exporting data in other formats. It's a common scenario for people who need to use or share datasets that can work with various online, financial, and scientific software programs.

Importing data into Excel

Spreadsheet programs can import many types of files, but there are three that turn up regularly:

➤ Comma-separated values (CSV).

➤ Tab-separated values (TSV).

➤ Text.

CSV files, which end in .csv, can be generated by financial, scientific, and engineering applications. They are text files that contain values (numbers or text) separated by commas. Because they are text files, they can be opened or edited in any text editor such as Notepad or TextEdit.

Many people encounter CSV files when they export data from their bank websites. CSV files then can be opened directly in Excel.

This is a sample of CSV data that I exported from a Google application, and then opened directly in Excel by double-clicking on the file:

	A	B	C	D	E	F
1	Chinese keyword adwords (Apr 11, 2013-Apr 17, 2013)					
2	Ad state	Ad	Description line 1	Description line 2	Display URL	Desti
3	enabled	Easy Chinese Dishes	In 30 Minutes, lea	Chinese food with	in30minutes	http:/
4	enabled	Simple Chinese Dishes	In 30 Minutes, lea	Chinese food with	in30minutes	http:/
5	enabled	Lazy Chinese Dishes	In 30 Minutes, lea	Chinese food with	in30minutes	http:/
6	enabled	30-minute Chinese Dishe	In 30 Minutes, lea	Chinese food with	in30minutes	http:/
7	enabled	Home-style Chinese Dish	In 30 Minutes, lea	Chinese food with	in30minutes	http:/
8	enabled	Easy Ingredients Chinese	In 30 Minutes, lea	Chinese food with	in30minutes	http:/

To open a CSV file on your hard drive in a new worksheet, go to *File > Open* and find the file on your hard drive (or online storage service such as One-Drive). You may be prompted to use the Text Import Wizard, described below.

To open a .csv file in Excel on an existing worksheet, follow these steps:

1. Create a blank file, or use a new worksheet.

2. Go to the Data ribbon and press the *Get External Data* button and select *From Text*.

3. Navigate to the folder containing the CSV file, which will appear as an Excel-compatible file.

4. Press the *Import* button. Excel's Text Import Wizard will guide you through selecting the appropriate options to convert it into a spreadsheet.

5. Make sure *Delimited* is checked in Step 1, and *Comma* is selected in Step 2.

6. Select *Finish*, then *OK*.

Here's what the Text Import Wizard looks like:

Google Sheets has a more straightforward process for importing CSV files, as well as other types of files. Simply go to *File > Import*, and you will be presented with various options for bringing in the data.

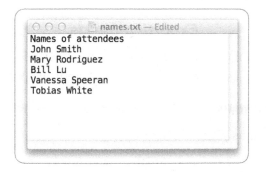

Tab-separated value (TSV) files are similar to CSV files. Instead of commas, tabbed inputs, which also can be created by pressing the Tab button on the keyboard, separate each piece of data.

Text files are useful for importing a single column of data. It might be a long list of names or a single column containing SKUs used for retail products. No special magic is needed to create such a file. Use a program like TextEdit (Mac) or Notepad (PC) and save the results as a .txt file. In the file, have one name on each line, with an optional header in the first line:

When the example is imported into a spreadsheet, each name will appear in a single cell in column A. If you wanted to import the first and last names into separate columns, you can still use TextEdit or Notepad, but save it as a CSV file. The data in the file would look like this:

```
○ ○ ○        names.csv — Edited
First name,Last name
John,Smith
Mary,Rodriguez
Bill,Lu
Vanessa,Speeran
Tobias,White
```

Exporting data

To export data from the active worksheet in Excel, follow these steps:

1. Go to *File > Save As* or *File > Export > Change File Type.*

2. Use the *Save As Type* menu at the bottom of the window to select the file type or data format.

The list of supported file types is long, and includes CSV and text. However, the most useful export format may actually be the native formats for Excel. Files ending in .xls or .xlsx are now accepted for import by other applications, including Microsoft Word, various database programs, and online services.

In Google Sheets, use *File > Download As* and select one of the available options, which include text, CSV, or .xlsx.

Exporting charts

Lastly, it's important to note that charts can be exported as image files. The .jpg, .gif, and .png files can then be used in all kinds of applications:

➤ Blogging software.

➤ Email programs (Outlook, Gmail, etc.).

➤ Word processors (Microsoft Word, Google Docs, etc.).

➤ Photo software (Apple Photos, Flickr, etc.).

➤ Presentation software (Microsoft PowerPoint, Google Slides, etc.).

To export a chart image, take the following steps:

Excel:

1. Select the chart and then press the copy icon on the Home ribbon.

2. Select the Paste button, and then select *Paste Special*.

3. In the pop-up window that appears, select the image format, such as *Picture (JPEG)*.

4. Right-click and select the *Save As* option to save the file on your hard drive or OneDrive.

5. Alternately, open Paint, Word, or other programs that support graphics and paste the image and then save it.

6. Excel Online does not support saving charts as image files. However, it is possible to use a screen capture program and then crop the image so just the chart is showing.

Google Sheets:

➤ Select on or near the top right edge of the chart until a small triangle appears. Activate it.

➤ Select *Save image*.

Collaboration and sharing

With the most recent versions of Excel and Excel Online, Microsoft has improved options to allow collaboration on shared documents. Google Drive and Google Sheets have more sophisticated collaboration options. Basic features are described below.

Excel:

How to share a spreadsheet file (no collaboration):

➤ *File > Share > Send Workbook* or *Send PDF* (requires desktop email to be configured).

➤ *File > Share > Copy View-Only Link* creates a URL that can be pasted into an email program, messaging application, or document. Recipients can view the file, but cannot edit it (requires spreadsheet file to be saved to OneDrive).

How to enable collaboration so more than one person can edit the document:

➤ *File > Share > Invite People* (requires spreadsheet file to be saved to OneDrive).

➤ *File > Share > Copy View and Edit Link* creates a URL that can be pasted into an email program, messaging application, or document (requires spreadsheet file to be saved to OneDrive).

Excel Online:

➤ *File > Share > Share with People* opens a wizard to share links with others (it is not necessary for link recipients to sign in to OneDrive to edit a shared spreadsheet file).

➤ *File > Share > Embed* allows spreadsheets to be embedded on a website.

Google Sheets:

Google has made it very easy to invite collaborators to work on a file or folder using email. Those who already have Google Accounts can begin to work on the shared file or folder right away. People who don't have Google Accounts will quickly be taken through the registration process. Non-collaborators will not be able to see the files.

To get started with collaboration using the Google Chrome browser or a Chromebook, confirm you are logged into your Google Account and have an active Internet connection. Then follow these steps:

1. Open the Sheets file.
2. Activate the *Share* button or go to *File > Share.*
3. The *Share with others* pop-up window will appear.
4. Enter the email addresses of collaborators in the *People* field.

5. Use the drop-down menu to the right of the field to control their access. This will determine if they can edit a document, add comments, or only view the contents.

6. To add a personal message to the notification email they receive, start typing in the *Add a note* field.

7. Press the *Done* button.

It's also possible to grant access to people who don't have Google Accounts or don't use email to share a document on the Web for anyone to see or edit. For more information about collaboration in Google Drive and Google Sheets, see Chapter 6 of *Google Drive & Docs In 30 Minutes.*

Chapter quiz

1. Why is landscape mode usually better for printing spreadsheets than portrait mode?

2. What export format is useful for determining what a printed worksheet will look like, without printing the file?

3. What are CSV files, and how do they relate to spreadsheet programs?

Answers can be seen in Appendix II on page 96

A message from the author

In a short period of time, you've learned the basics of Excel. You've gone from simple definitions to step-by-step explanations of how to use functions, make charts, and sort data. This knowledge can be applied to the workplace, school, and even at home.

While the lessons and terminology are still fresh in your mind, it's a good idea to play around with an actual spreadsheet and commit some of the basics to memory. I've uploaded some sample spreadsheets to the official companion website to *Excel Basics In 30 Minutes*, located at *excel.in30minutes.com*. The files are free to download, and include the worksheets that were used as examples throughout this guide. Even if you don't have Excel installed on your computer, you can practice your spreadsheet skills by creating a Google Account (see Appendix I) and trying Google Sheets.

In addition, I have created quick-reference cheat sheets for both Excel 2016 and Google Sheets. They contain tips, examples, lists of keyboard shortcuts, and other resources. They are available as printed four-panel pamphlets or downloadable PDFs. Visit in30minutes.com/cheatsheets for more information.

I also have a request. Could you take a minute to rate *Excel Basics In 30 Minutes (2nd Edition)* and write a quick online review? An honest appraisal of the contents of *Excel Basics In 30 Minutes* will not only be appreciated by me, but it will also let other potential readers know what to expect.

Thanks for reading!

Ian Lamont

About the author

Excel Basics In 30 Minutes (2nd Edition) is authored by Ian Lamont, an award-winning business and technology journalist and founder of IN 30 MINUTES guides. Lamont has written for more than a dozen online and print publications and has also served as the managing editor of *The Industry Standard*. He has written several IN 30 MINUTES guides, including *Dropbox In 30 Minutes*, *Google Drive & Docs In 30 Minutes*, and *Twitter In 30 Minutes*.

Lamont is a graduate of the Boston University College of Communication and MIT's Sloan Fellows program. He lives with his family in the Boston area.

Glossary

AutoFill–An Excel feature that lets users quickly fill in a series of values across cells without having to type formulas or functions in every cell.

Cell–Visually represented by rectangles and referenced by a combination of letters and numbers (for instance, F2); cells can contain numbers, text, functions, or formulas. Cells can be added together, merged, or formatted.

Comma-separated value (CSV)–These are text files (ending with the suffix .csv) that are generated by certain financial, scientific, and engineering applications. CSV files contain values (numbers or text) separated by commas.

Formula–A mathematical formula entered into a cell, starting with an equal sign. A simple addition formula would be *=A1+A2*.

Formula Bar–Displays the formula or function for the selected cell.

Function–A code starting with an equal sign that performs a mathematical operation on a cell or group of cells (such as multiplication) or transforms the values or contents in some way. Example: *=SUM(A3:A5)* adds the contents of the cells A3, A4, and A5.

Mathematical operation–Includes addition, multiplication, subtraction, and division, as well as more advanced operations.

PEMDAS–Parentheses, Exponents, Multiplication, Division, Addition, and Subtraction. PEMDAS determines which mathematical operations to perform first.

Workbook–Microsoft's term for a spreadsheet file.

Worksheet–A page in a spreadsheet file, containing a grid of cells.

Registering for Google Sheets

Google Sheets is a free online spreadsheets program that is part of Google's online office suite. To use it, you first need to sign up for a Google Account. This takes seconds to set up, and the requirements are simple. All you need to do is provide an email address and answer a few basic questions online. No discs or downloads are needed!

Go to *drive.google.com* to get started. If you already have a Gmail account, use your credentials to log in. Otherwise, look for a link or button to create a new account. You'll be brought to the Google Account registration screen (Google Accounts are required for certain Google services, such as Google Drive, Google Docs, Google Sheets, Gmail, and Google Calendar). Then follow these steps:

1. Enter a first and last name. Note that the name you enter will be associated with any content you create or share on any Google services, including YouTube videos, app and product reviews on Google Play, and shared Google Drive folders and files. If you are not comfortable using your real name in these situations, use an alternative first and last name.

2. In the next field, type a username that will become your new Gmail address. Or, select "I prefer to use my current email address" and enter an existing email address that you want to associate with Google Drive and other Google services. It can be any working email address, including Yahoo Mail, Aol.com, or your work email. If the username is already registered, you will be asked to create a new one.

3. Enter a password (minimum of 8 characters long).

4. Enter your birthday. This is required. If you don't want to use your actual DOB, make one up—it's your chance to be 21 again!

5. Enter your gender. This is mandatory, although if you are uncomfortable with this step you can choose "Other."

6. *Mobile Phone* is an optional field. I recommend entering a real mobile number here, as this can help prevent other people from taking control of your account—Google will use the number to verify you are the actual owner in case someone attempts to log in to Google Drive from a new computer.

7. Enter a series of numbers and/or letters to prove to Google that you are human (this helps prevent malicious computer programs from signing up for Google services and spreading spam).

8. Select your location.

9. Agree to Google's Privacy Policy and Terms of Service, and select the *Next Step* button.

10. If you've done everything right, you'll be taken to a confirmation page.

If you've done everything right, you'll be taken to a confirmation page. Check your inbox for the confirmation message that Google sent you, and select the link to activate your Google account. You must do this to use Google Sheets as well as Google Drive, where your spreadsheets will be stored.

Return to *drive.google.com*, and log on with your email address and the password you created. On the next screen, you'll see something like this:

The *New* button is where most of the action for Google Drive takes place. Pressing New will display options for creating various types of files, including new spreadsheets in Google Sheets.

Once you've created a file in Google Sheets, you can rename it and start entering data. It will be saved automatically. Close the browser window to close the file. All of your Google Sheets files can accessed via drive.google.com.

Quiz answers

The four main chapters of this book featured short quizzes to test your knowledge. Some questions require the use of Excel or Google Sheets to answer.

Quiz answers: Chapter 1

Recommended answer to #1:

Place the values in a column A, starting with cell A1.

Option 1: Enter the following formula in cell A5:

=A1+A2+A3+A4

Option 2: Enter the following formula in cell A5:

=SUM(A1:A4)

Option 3: Use AutoSum (Excel only)

Answer to #2:

1. Highlight B2, B3, and B4.
2. Press the drop-down menu icon next to the Sigma symbol.
3. Choose *AVERAGE()*. The results will be shown in cell B5.

Answer to #3:

1. Highlight the cells that need to have their background colors changed.
2. Press the *Fill* button on the Home ribbon.
3. Select the color you want to use for the background.

Quiz answers: Chapter 2

Answer for #1:

=1023*9.12

Answer for #2:

Format the cell for percentages, using the % button or equivalent menu item.

Recommended answer for #3:

In row 1, create six column headers starting with the year 2017. Cell A2 contains the starting amount for 2017 ($10,000) while the remaining cells in row 2 will contain the balance after compounding. Cell A3 contains the interest rate (5%).

In 2018, the new balance will be $10,000+5%. Using our cell references, the formula in cell B2 will be:

=A2*(1+$A$3)

Then drag cell B2 to the right until every year has a value. By the end of the fifth year of the CD, the final value will be displayed—$12,763.

This example assumes no additional fees or taxes.

Recommended answer for #4:

Column A contains the names of the people, column B contains their approximate weights, and column C will contain the converted weight. For the weights in column B, just type the number value—do not add "pounds" or "kilos" to the cells. Cell E2 contains the value "2.2", which is the number that is used to convert between pounds and kilograms.

If you are converting from pounds to kilograms, you need to divide the weight for each person by 2.2. For the first person, use the fixed cell reference and create this formula in cell C2:

=B2/$E$2

Press *Return/Enter*, and then select the cell and drag it down column C to convert the other weights.

If you are converting from kilograms to pounds, you need to multiply the values in column B by 2.2, starting with the following formula in cell C2:

=B2*$E$2

After pressing *Return/Enter*, select the cell and drag it down to convert the remaining weights in column C.

You can also have the conversion take place without the fixed cell reference (for instance, "*=B2*2.2*").

Quiz answers: Chapter 3

Answer for #1:

Select all cells and sort column B (which contains their last names) in ascending order.

Answer for #2:

Filter the results for column D, and create a rule that only includes values that are equal to or less than 60.

Answer for #3:

If only one column is selected, then only that data will be sorted—meaning the other columns will no longer match up. For instance, using the high school example in question #1, if only the column with last names were selected for the sort operation, then the first names, ages, and grades would no longer match up with the correct last name.

Quiz answers: Chapter 4

Answer to #1:

In portrait mode, columns often get cut off. Landscape mode is better able to preserve worksheets with more columns.

Answer to #2:

PDFs.

Answer to #3:

CSV stands for *comma-separated value*. It's a text file, with each row of data containing individual values separated by commas. CSV files are created by other applications, but can be imported into spreadsheet programs. Spreadsheet programs such as Microsoft Excel can also generate CSV files.

Index

Introduction to
Google Drive & Docs
In 30 Minutes

The following bonus chapter is the introduction to Google Drive & Docs In 30 Minutes (2nd Edition). To download the ebook or purchase the paperback, visit the book's official website, googledrive.in30minutes.com.

Why you need to use Google's free office suite

Thanks for picking up a copy of *Google Drive & Docs In 30 Minutes,* 2nd Edition. I wrote this unofficial user guide to help people get up to speed with Google's remarkable (and free) online office suite that includes file storage (Google Drive), a word processor (Google Docs), a spreadsheet program (Google Sheets), and a presentation tool (Google Slides).

How do people use these applications? There are many possible uses. Consider these examples:

> ➤ **A harried product manager needs to work on an important proposal over the weekend.** In the past, she would have dug around in her purse to look for an old USB drive she uses for transferring files. Or, she might have emailed herself an attachment to open at home. Not anymore. Now she saves the Word document and an Excel spreadsheet to Google Drive at the office. Later that evening, on her home PC, she opens her Google Drive folder to access and edit the files. All of her saves are updated to Google Drive. When she returns to work the following Monday, the updated data can be viewed at her workstation.

> ➤ **The organizer of a family reunion wants to survey 34 cousins** about attendance, lodging preferences, and potluck dinner preparation (always a challenge—the Nebraska branch of the family won't eat corn or Garbanzo beans). He emails everyone a link to an online form he created using Google Forms. Relatives open the form on their browsers, and submit their answers. The answers are automatically transferred to Sheets, where the organizer can see the responses and tally the results.

> ➤ A small business consultant is helping the owner of Slappy's Canadian Diner ("*We Put The Canadian Back In Bacon*") **prepare a slideshow for potential franchisees in Ohio**. The consultant and Slappy collaborate using Google Slides, which lets them remotely access the deck and add text, images, and other elements. The consultant shares a link to the slideshow with her consulting partner, so he can periodically review it on the Google Slides app on his phone and check for problems. Later,

Slappy meets his potential franchise operators at a hotel in Cleveland, and uses Google Slides on his iPad to pitch his business.

➤ **An elementary school faculty uses Docs to collaborate on lesson plans.** Each teacher accesses the same document from home or the classroom. Updates are instantly reflected, even when two teachers are simultaneously accessing the same document. Their principal (known as "Skinner" behind his back) is impressed by how quickly the faculty completes the plans, and how well the curriculums are integrated.

➤ At the same school, the 5th-grade teachers **ask their students to submit homework using Docs**. The teachers add corrections and notes, which the students can access at home using a Web browser. It's much more efficient than emailing attachments, and the students don't need to bug their parents to purchase Microsoft Office.

Many people are introduced to Google's online office suite through Docs, the incredibly popular online word processor. Others are attracted by the free storage and syncing features of Google Drive. Microsoft Office, which includes Word, Excel, PowerPoint, and OneDrive, can cost hundreds of dollars. While Drive is not as sophisticated as Microsoft Office, it handles basic documents and spreadsheets very well. Google Drive also offers a slew of powerful online features, including:

➤ The ability to review the history of a specific document, and revert to an earlier version.

➤ Simple Web forms and online surveys which can be produced without programming skills or website hosting arrangements.

➤ Collaboration features that let users work on the same document in real time.

➤ Offline file storage that can be synced to multiple computers.

➤ Automatic notification of the release date of Brad Pitt's next movie.

I'm just kidding about the last item. But Google Drive, Docs, Sheets, Forms, and Slides really can do those other things, and without the help of your company's IT department or the pimply teenager from down the street.

These features are built right into the software, and are ready to use as soon as you've signed up.

Even though the myriad features of Google's office suite may seem overwhelming, this guide makes it easy to get started. *Google Drive & Docs In 30 Minutes* is written in plain English, with lots of step-by-step instructions, screenshots and tips. More resources are available on the companion website to this book, *googledrive.in30minutes.com*. You'll get up to speed in no time.

The second edition of *Google Drive & Docs In 30 Minutes* covers interface improvements that Google rolled out in late 2014 and 2015, as well as the expanded capabilities of the Google Drive, Docs, Sheets, and Slides apps for iOS and Android.

We've only got half an hour, so let's get started. If you are using a PC or laptop, please download the Google Chrome browser, which works best with Google Drive, Docs, Slides, and Sheets. Instructions for the Chromebook and the mobile apps are referenced throughout the guide.

If you're interested in learning more about this title, or buying the ebook or paperback, visit the official website located at googledrive.in30minutes.com.